WITHDRAWN

Parade of Popular Hits

A READER'S DIGEST SONGBOOK

Editor: William L. Simon
Music arranged and edited by Dan Fox
Senior Staff Editor: Mary Kelleher
Associate Editor: Natalie Moreda
Designer: Judy Skorpil
Music Associate: Elizabeth Mead
Annotated by Jim Lowe
Illustrations by Cameron Wasson

READER'S DIGEST GENERAL BOOKS
Editor in Chief: John A. Pope, Jr.
Managing Editor: Jane Polley
Art Director: David Trooper
Group Editors: Norman B. Mack, Susan J. Wernert,
Joel Musler *(Art)*
Chief of Research: Monica Borrowman
Copy Chief: Edward W. Atkinson
Picture Editor: Robert J. Woodward
Rights and Permissions: Pat Colomban
Head Librarian: Jo Manning

THE READER'S DIGEST ASSOCIATION, INC.
Pleasantville, New York/Montreal

Reader's Digest Fund for the Blind is publisher of
the Large-Type Edition of *Reader's Digest.* For
subscription information about this magazine,
please contact Reader's Digest Fund for the Blind,
Inc., Dept. 250, Pleasantville, N.Y. 10570.

INTRODUCTION

In the years between April 1935 and April 1959, the world may have been at its worst. In 1935, Hitler and Stalin were in power and the Great Depression was raging; ahead lay the Spanish Civil War, World War II, the Cold War in Europe and the hot war in Korea. And yet, ironically enough, in the midst of all the turmoil, American popular music flourished as never before...Fred and Ginger, Der Bingle, Betty Grable, the Big Band Era, Frank Sinatra, Hollywood and Broadway at their best.

But why those seemingly arbitrary dates—April 1935?...April 1959? Well, they constitute the boundaries—the birth, life and death—of *Your Hit Parade*. And if you can remember rumble seats in cars and bank nights at movie palaces, you will certainly recall that sensational radio-television program. Saturday night and *Your Hit Parade* were synonymous. Lean back in your chair, close your eyes and listen. Can't you hear those two tobacco auctioneers, F.E. Boone and L.A. "Speed" Riggs, chanting at the beginning of each show? Why the tobacco auctioneers? Because *Your Hit Parade* was sponsored by Lucky Strike cigarettes, back in the days when more people smoked than didn't smoke and cigarette ads hadn't yet been banned from the airwaves.

Your Hit Parade was a compilation of the most popular tunes of each week, determined by the number of times a song was played on the air, its record and sheet music sales, and, as the announcer André Baruch would say, the number of times it had been played on "automatic coin machines"—apparently he couldn't bring himself to say "jukeboxes." And through the years, the country's top songs were sung by many of the country's top singers on the Columbia Broadcasting System's top musical program.

And what songs! To start with, there were the big Hollywood studios—MGM, Paramount, Warner Brothers, Twentieth Century-Fox, RKO, Columbia—turning out dozens of film musicals each year, each one packed with dazzling melodies by the likes of Irving Berlin, Jerome Kern, Cole Porter, Harry Warren, the Gershwins, Johnny Mercer, Jimmy Van Heusen, Johnny Burke and Sammy Cahn. So great was the flow of glorious tunes and lyrics that some of the standards we still hear and love today weren't even nominated for an Academy Award!

Then there was Broadway—the Broadway of Rodgers and Hart, of Rodgers and Hammerstein, of Burton Lane and E.Y. Harburg, Alan Jay Lerner and Frederick Loewe, and Frank Loesser. The Broadway of such shows as *On Your Toes, The Boys from Syracuse, Oklahoma!, Carousel, Finian's Rainbow, Guys and Dolls* and *My Fair Lady*. So many of them—even shows that themselves flopped—supplied *Your Hit Parade* with songs we cherish today.

On top of that were the glorious big bands—those of Glenn Miller, Tommy and Jimmy Dorsey, and Artie Shaw among them—all hungry for great songs, not only from films and shows but also from Tin Pan Alley, songs written to stand on their own, without a Broadway stage or the silver screen to serve as an incubator.

Parade of Popular Hits is Reader's Digest's 13th music book. In those earlier 12 books are more than 1,000 songs, many of which were written during this great musical era. And now here are 92 more standard-bearers in that marvelous parade of American popular music. Most of them came out between 1935 and 1959 and were on *Your Hit Parade*. In addition to being wonderful songs, they are easy to sing and easy to play, in large part due to Dan Fox's arrangements. As always, Dan has done a superb job of making them facile yet exciting. Play them, sing them, enjoy them. One wishes that the flow of wonderful melodies we heard every week could have gone on forever.

But, alas, nothing is forever. Maybe it was just too good to last. In any event, *Your Hit Parade* finally went off the air, and with it, the beautiful tunes it presented. Gone—but, thank heavens, not forgotten—were songs like "Moonlight Becomes You," "I Let a Song Go Out of My Heart," "Because of You," "Ebb Tide," "And the Angels Sing," "I Won't Dance," "A Fine Romance," "That Old Black Magic," "How About You?," "Blue Orchids" and "But Beautiful." Here they are now for your enjoyment.

They are but beautiful, indeed. And their melodies linger on.

— The Editors

HOW TO USE THIS BOOK

As in all of our music books, the arrangements in *Parade of Popular Hits* were designed to be easy to play while still being musically interesting and artistically gratifying. For players of any treble clef instrument, the melody is on top, clear and uncluttered, with the stems of the notes turned up. However, if one plays in tandem with a piano or organ, it must be on a "C" instrument, such as a violin, flute, recorder, oboe, accordion, harmonica, melodica or any of the new electronic keyboards. Guitarists can also play the melody as written, or they can play chords from the symbols (G7, Am, etc.) or from the diagrams printed just above the staves. Organists whose instruments have foot pedals may use the *small* pedal notes in the bass clef (with stems turned down). *But these pedal notes should not be attempted by pianists;* they are for feet only! For the sake of facility, the pedal lines move stepwise and stay within an octave. Players who improvise in the jazz sense can "take off" from the melody and the chord symbols.

The chord symbols also are designed for pianists who have studied the popular chord method; players can read the melody line and improvise their own left-hand accompaniments. The chord symbols may be used, too, by bass players (string or brass); just play the root note of each chord symbol, except where another note is indicated (for example, "D/F♯ bass"). Accordionists can use the chord symbols for the left-hand buttons while playing the treble portions of the arrangement as written.

ABOUT JIM LOWE

Jim Lowe, who supplied the colorful annotations for the songs in Parade of Popular Hits, *is a veteran of New York dio. For many years, the "King of Trivia" held forth on* The Jim Lowe Music Hall *on WNEW-AM as an eloquent spokesman for the cause of quality popular music.*

INDEX TO SECTIONS

INDEX TO SONGS

7AV

WHERE THE BLUE OF THE NIGHT

(MEETS THE GOLD OF THE DAY)

Some theme songs are so closely associated with a performer that the very mention of the song conjures up the person. "I'm Gettin' Sentimental Over You" suggests Tommy Dorsey; "When the Moon Comes Over the Mountain," Kate Smith. What is there to say about "Where the Blue of the Night" except what you already know: it

served Bing Crosby steadily and well, on radio and television, for many years. It was performed at the beginning of every Crosby broadcast and—unless Bing had spent too much time ad-libbing with too many guests—at the end of the program as well. The charming song seems somehow to convey Crosby's warmth, dignity and perspective, and it remains a wonderful memory of the man.

Words and Music by Roy Turk, Bing Crosby and Fred E. Ahlert

Slow, sentimental waltz

Where the blue of the night meets the gold of the day, Some-one waits for me.____ And the gold of her hair crowns the blue of her eyes Like a

Bing Crosby borrowed this song from another of Hollywood's brightest stars, the legendary Judy Garland, who sang it in *The Harvey Girls*, one of Metro-Goldwyn-Mayer's big, splashy musicals. Miss Garland, fresh from her rousing success in *Meet Me in St. Louis*, was supplied a lilting score by two of filmdom's best songwriters, Johnny Mercer and Harry Warren. Actually, the movie marked a reunion for the two men. They had teamed up at Warner Brothers in 1938–39 on big back-to-back hits: "You Must Have Been a Beautiful Baby" and "Jeepers Creepers," both No. 1 songs on *Your Hit Parade*. "On the Atchison, Topeka and the Santa Fe" didn't make No. 1, but it got as high as second place and stayed in the Top 10 for 14 weeks in 1945. More important, it went on to win the Academy Award as Best Song of 1946. It has been recorded by many people through the years, but Bing's and Judy's versions remain the highlights.

From *The Harvey Girls*   Words by Johnny Mercer; Music by Harry Warren

MOONLIGHT BECOMES YOU

"Moonlight Becomes You" is a product of the great team of Johnny Burke and Jimmy Van Heusen. It is also one of the many standards that were born "on the road," so to speak. It first saw the light of day in the 1942 film *Road to Morocco* — the third of the Bing Crosby-Bob Hope-Dorothy Lamour *Road* shows—and it became No. 1 on *Your Hit Parade* shortly thereafter. To this day, it remains one of the most enduring and hauntingly beautiful of American popular songs. Bing's persona was on such a lofty plane that in a song he seldom came right out and said "I love you." In some strange way, that would have compromised his image. This beating around the bush is exemplified in "Moonlight Becomes You": "If I say I love you, I want you to know." That was a big "if," and it was about as close as Der Bingle ever came to total commitment in a song.

From *Road to Morocco*
Words by Johnny Burke; Music by Jimmy Van Heusen

Moon-light be-comes you; It goes with your hair. You cer-tain-ly know the right thing to wear.

SWEET AND LOVELY

This song, like so many of the beautiful Bing Crosby ballads, dates back to the early years of his unprecedented career. The tune was written in part by Gus Arnheim, one of the West Coast's top bandleaders. In the Los Angeles of the late 1920s and early 1930s, with its Cocoanut Grove and Biltmore Bowl and other watering holes, several well-known bands were in residence, and Arnheim's was probably the best known. Among the reasons were some excellent musicians and, at different times, Arnheim's male vocalists Bing Crosby and Russ Columbo. Arnheim was also a songwriter of considerable note, having co-written two of the biggest and best songs of the 1920s and early 1930s, "Sweet and Lovely" (which enjoyed a big revival in the 1940s) and "I Cried for You."

Words and Music by Gus Arnheim, Harry Tobias and Jules Lemare

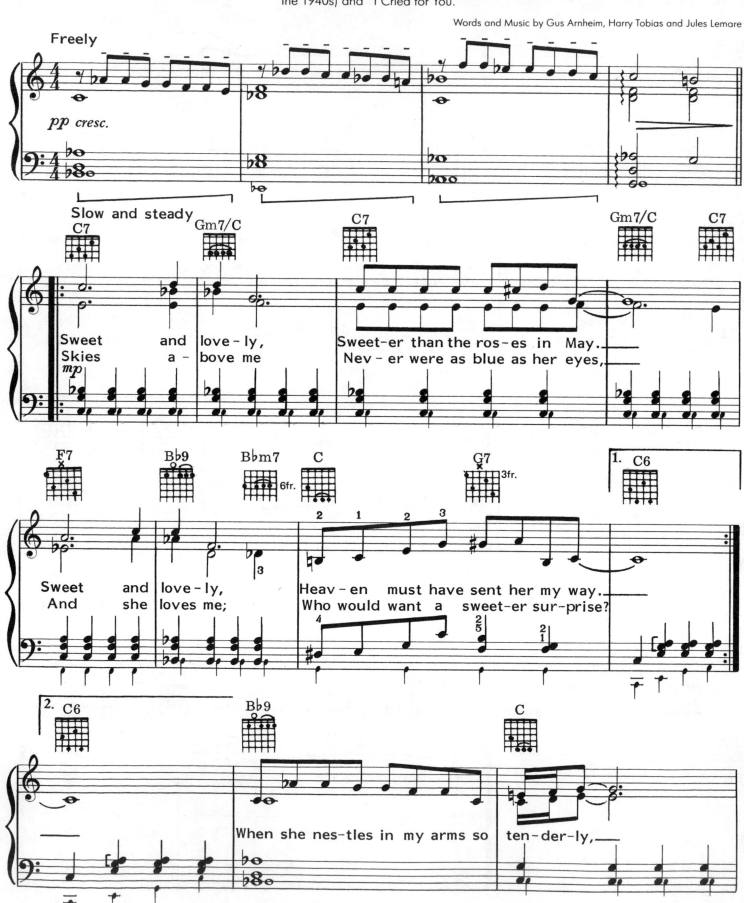

Sweet and love-ly, Sweet-er than the ros-es in May.
Skies a-bove me Nev-er were as blue as her eyes,

Sweet and love-ly, Heav-en must have sent her my way.
And she loves me; Who would want a sweet-er sur-prise?

When she nes-tles in my arms so ten-der-ly,—

There's a thrill that words can-not ex-press.
In my heart a song of love is
taunt-ing me,___ Mel-o - dy haunt-ing me.
Sweet and love-ly, Sweet-er than the ros-es in May.___
And she loves me; There is noth-ing more I can say.

slowing

in tempo

LOVE IS JUST AROUND THE CORNER

Leo Robin and Ralph Rainger wrote some of Bing Crosby's biggest early-career hits, including "Please," "June in January" and "Love in Bloom." However, Rainger apparently was elsewhere employed when "Love Is Just Around the Corner" was written for the 1935 film *Here Is My Heart*. In the movie, Bing, playing—what else?—a crooner, pretends he's a waiter so that he can get close to an aloof princess (Kitty Carlisle) whom he adores. One of the studio's directors, Lewis Gensler, wrote the melody for the perky song, which turned out to be one of Crosby's bigger hits of the period. It had some sparkling Robin lyrics, including the very witty "But strictly between us, you're cuter than Venus, and what's more you've got arms." Rainger was only 42 when he died in 1942, but Robin, who passed away in 1984, continued to have a most successful career, both in Hollywood and on Broadway. He wrote the lyrics to the tunes of Jule Styne for *Gentlemen Prefer Blondes* and, in the 1970s, contributed to a follow-up to that hit, called *Lorelei*.

From *Here Is My Heart*
Words and Music by Leo Robin and Lewis E. Gensler

With an easy swing

Love is just a-round the cor-ner, An-y co-zy lit-tle cor-ner. Love is just a-round the cor - ner___ When

Wrap your troubles in dreams

In his autobiography, *Call Me Lucky,* Bing Crosby tells of motoring down the Pacific Coast in 1925 from his native state of Washington. His driving (and singing) companion was a fellow named Al Rinker. When their car broke down on the outskirts of Los Angeles, Rinker's sister, Mildred Bailey, rescued them and took them into her home. Already an established singer, she was able to help them profes-

sionally, and for a while all three of them sang with Paul Whiteman's orchestra at the same time. By then, Bing and Al had been joined by a third singer, Harry Barris, in a trio they called The Rhythm Boys. Barris was also a songwriter, and one can only assume that it was more than coincidence that Bing recorded "Wrap Your Troubles in Dreams" and several other Barris compositions early in his career.

Words by Ted Koehler and Billy Moll; Music by Harry Barris

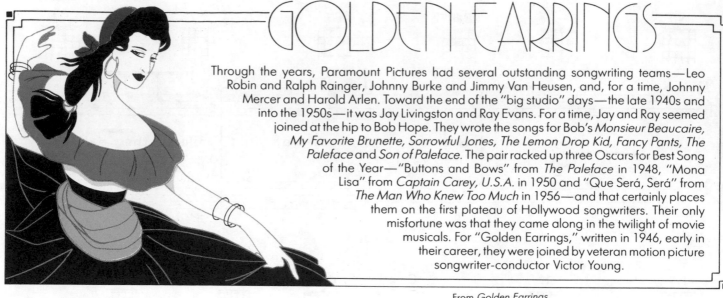

GOLDEN EARRINGS

Through the years, Paramount Pictures had several outstanding songwriting teams—Leo Robin and Ralph Rainger, Johnny Burke and Jimmy Van Heusen, and, for a time, Johnny Mercer and Harold Arlen. Toward the end of the "big studio" days—the late 1940s and into the 1950s—it was Jay Livingston and Ray Evans. For a time, Jay and Ray seemed joined at the hip to Bob Hope. They wrote the songs for Bob's *Monsieur Beaucaire*, *My Favorite Brunette*, *Sorrowful Jones*, *The Lemon Drop Kid*, *Fancy Pants*, *The Paleface* and *Son of Paleface*. The pair racked up three Oscars for Best Song of the Year—"Buttons and Bows" from *The Paleface* in 1948, "Mona Lisa" from *Captain Carey, U.S.A.* in 1950 and "Que Será, Será" from *The Man Who Knew Too Much* in 1956—and that certainly places them on the first plateau of Hollywood songwriters. Their only misfortune was that they came along in the twilight of movie musicals. For "Golden Earrings," written in 1946, early in their career, they were joined by veteran motion picture songwriter-conductor Victor Young.

From *Golden Earrings*
Words by Jay Livingston and Ray Evans; Music by Victor Young

BUT BEAUTIFUL

Bing Crosby and Bob Hope made seven *Road* movies. They first hit the pavement—or sometimes dirt paths—in 1940 with *Road to Singapore* and last in the 1960s with *Road to Hong Kong*. Their co-star in the first six films was the Sarong Girl, sultry Dorothy Lamour. But by the time the boys reached Hong Kong, Dorothy's role had been reduced to a cameo, and in that last one in their dynasty they appeared opposite a young lady who would have her own *Dynasty* a couple of decades later. That's right—Joan Collins, the infamous Alexis of the television series. In between Singapore and Hong Kong, Paramount gave Bing and Bob and Dorothy the maps to Zanzibar, Morocco, Utopia, Rio and Bali. Each stop they made during the 1940s, a gold-mine era of great lyrics and music, contained some of that studio's greatest songs. Most of these tunes were written by one of Hollywood's most prolific and talented twosomes, Johnny Burke and Jimmy Van Heusen. This particular one is from the 1947 *Road to Rio*, the cast of which also included those Queens of the Jukebox, The Andrews Sisters. And "But Beautiful" it is.

From *Road to Rio*
Words by Johnny Burke; Music by Jimmy Van Heusen

JUST FRIENDS

The three reigning baritones of the early 1930s were Bing Crosby, Rudy Vallee and Russ Columbo. Vallee would go on to sustained success, not as a singer but as the emcee and guiding spirit of one of the first network radio variety shows, *The Fleischmann Hour*. Under various sponsorships, he remained a favorite for many years in those pre-television days. In the 1940s, his heartthrob years a distant memory, he became a film foil and excellent light comedian in such hit movies as *The Palm Beach Story*. The story of Russ Columbo was ill-starred indeed. The handsome young Italian-American's singing and film careers were cut short tragically when he shot himself while cleaning a gun. There were those who said that had he lived he would have become the screen's next great lover. Once where there were three, now there was just Bing Crosby.

Words by Sam H. Lewis; Music by John Klenner

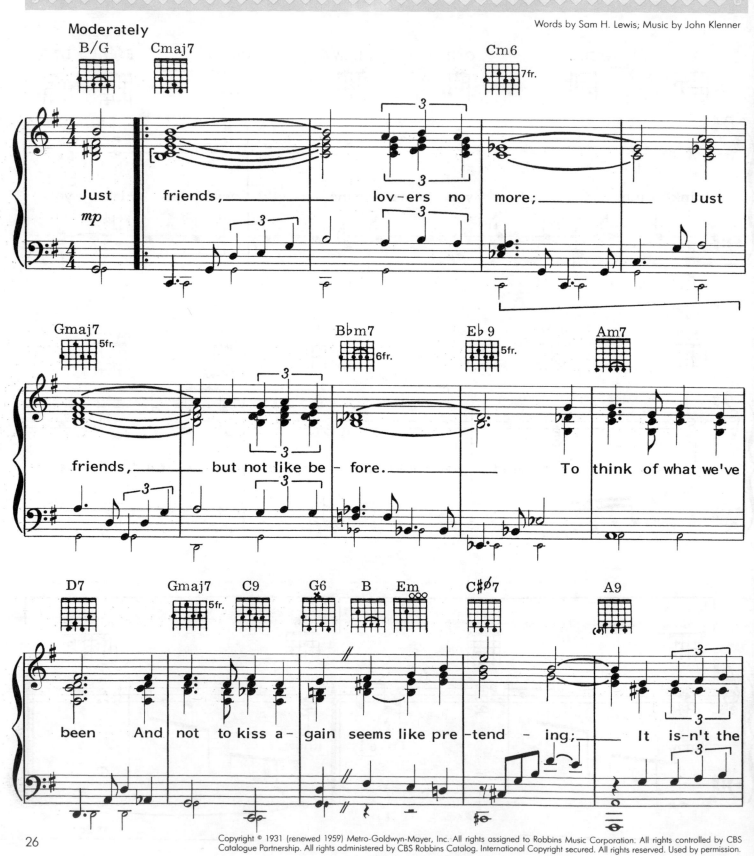

LOVE IN BLOOM

Here is a Bing Crosby song that got out of hand—way out of hand. Bing introduced the pretty ballad innocently enough in a 1934 motion picture called *She Loves Me Not,* in which he had two leading ladies, Miriam Hopkins and Kitty Carlisle. It was one of those college musicals in which Paramount frequently found itself involved. In fact, Bing had co-starred with George Burns and Gracie Allen just the previous year in a movie of the same genre called *College Humor.* Somehow or other, that vicious violin virtuoso Jack Benny soon got a hold (a stranglehold) on "Love in Bloom," and it—and the public— was never the same again. That infamous sound still comes squeaking down the corridors of time from countless radio and television shows of the world's most famous (and beloved) miser. Benny got a lot of mileage out of the song, and its writers, Leo Robin and Ralph Rainger, must have laughed *and* cried all the way to the bank after the comedian destroyed it as a serious ballad.

From *She Loves Me Not*
Words and Music by Leo Robin and Ralph Rainger

Can it be the trees that fill the breeze with rare and mag-ic per-fume? Oh, no, it is-n't the trees; It's love in bloom.

HOW ABOUT YOU?

By the time Judy Garland, an established MGM star, sang this song, she had already been in love with Andy Hardy and had traveled the yellow brick road to Oz. She and Mickey Rooney introduced "How About You?" in the 1941 film *Babes on Broadway*. The great Burton Lane composed the music. The lyrics were written by Ralph Freed, whose brother Arthur headed the MGM musical film division during its glory years. So if ever there was a born-and-bred MGM song, this is it. "How About You?" was nominated for an Oscar for Best Film Song of the Year, but, as Burton said, "We had a little trouble winning it. Ran into a song called 'White Christmas.'"

Words by Ralph Freed; Music by Burton Lane

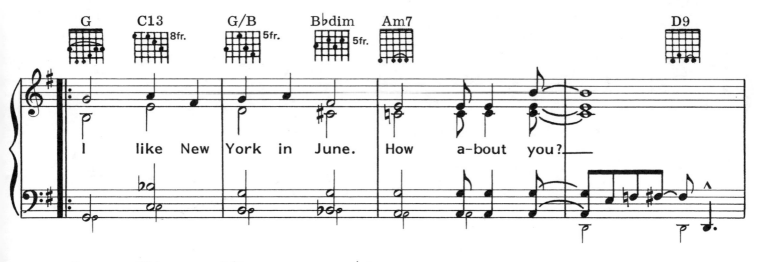

I like New York in June. How a-bout you?

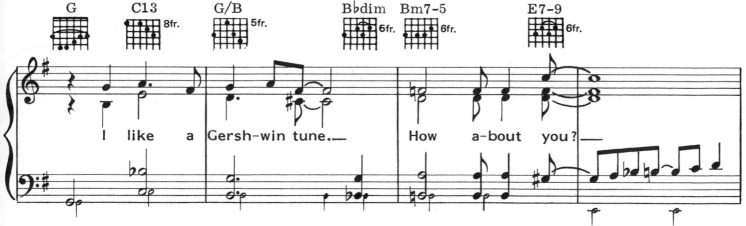

I like a Gersh-win tune.— How a-bout you?—

One can only wonder what songwriters would have done without the moon. Perhaps they would have had to invent one. Shining away up there in the sky, the moon appears in the title of literally hundreds of American popular songs, not to mention its place in the lyrics of countless others. It shone brightly over Tin Pan Alley from the early part of this century until the arrival of rock and roll, whose followers seem more attracted to the light of neon and strobe. Musically, the moon has hovered over Burma, Miami, the Carolinas, the Mississippi, the Ganges, the Hudson, the Missouri, Manakoora, London, Monterey, Hawaii, the Alamo and Cuba. It used to be said that the sun never set on the British Empire. Well, for almost as many years, the moon never set on Tin Pan Alley, where most of New York City's songwriters and publishers hung their cadenzas.

Words and Music by Mack David, Mack Davis and André Kostelanetz
Based on Tchaikovsky's Fifth Symphony, Second Movement Theme

Once in a While

"Once in a While," co-written by Bud Green and Michael Edwards, was one of Tommy Dorsey's biggest hits. In fact, across the country in the late '30s, rare indeed was the jukebox that didn't house Dorsey's recording, with Jack Leonard's excellent, soft vocal — backed by a pre-Pied Piper group of singers — giving it just the sentimental but not cloying touch it required. Due to the record, the song made the No. 1 spot on *Your Hit Parade* on November 27, 1937, and remained in that position for seven straight weeks.

Words by Bud Green; Music by Michael Edwards

In the Blue of Evening

After a few months singing with the Harry James band, Frank Sinatra joined the Tommy Dorsey organization in January 1940, and the world of popular music was never quite the same again. Sinatra's singing immediately served notice that the boy-singer space with T.D. belonged exclusively to him. This beautiful song, written by a radio conductor named Alfonso D'Artega, was one of the last that he recorded with Dorsey. The date was June 17, 1942. Just around the corner for Frank was the Paramount Theater . . . and the Big Time.

Words by Tom Adair; Music by Alfonso A. D'Artega

ie._____

In the blue of eve-ning,

While crick-ets call

And stars are fall-ing,_____

There neath the star – lit

sky   You'll come to me._____

Evenly, with a lilt

In the shad-ows of the night we'll stand; I'll touch your hand and then

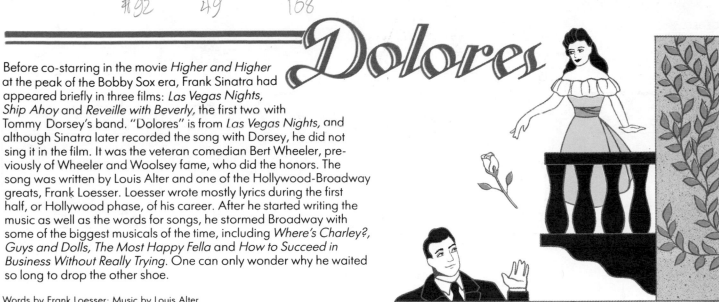

Dolores

Before co-starring in the movie *Higher and Higher* at the peak of the Bobby Sox era, Frank Sinatra had appeared briefly in three films: *Las Vegas Nights,* *Ship Ahoy* and *Reveille with Beverly,* the first two with Tommy Dorsey's band. "Dolores" is from *Las Vegas Nights,* and although Sinatra later recorded the song with Dorsey, he did not sing it in the film. It was the veteran comedian Bert Wheeler, previously of Wheeler and Woolsey fame, who did the honors. The song was written by Louis Alter and one of the Hollywood-Broadway greats, Frank Loesser. Loesser wrote mostly lyrics during the first half, or Hollywood phase, of his career. After he started writing the music as well as the words for songs, he stormed Broadway with some of the biggest musicals of the time, including *Where's Charley?,* *Guys and Dolls, The Most Happy Fella* and *How to Succeed in Business Without Really Trying.* One can only wonder why he waited so long to drop the other shoe.

Words by Frank Loesser; Music by Louis Alter

* Attention - Guitarists and all chord method players:
The simplified harmonies represented by these symbols and diagrams cannot be played together with this special keyboard arrangement.

OH! YOU CRAZY MOON

Tommy Dorsey and his slightly older brother Jimmy arrived in New York from their native Scranton in the late 1920s, and — like so many other future big-band greats — went to work in recording studios, in the pit orchestras of Broadway shows and at the radio networks. The brothers started their own band but eventually went their separate ways, with Jimmy forming a band that came to be centered around the boy-girl combination of singers Bob Eberly and Helen O'Connell, and Tommy developing what many observers feel was the best band of them all. This strong ballad was one of Tommy's big hits.

With an easy lilting swing

Words by Johnny Burke; Music by Jimmy Van Heusen

When they met, the way they smiled, I saw that I was through.
When they kissed, they tried to say That it was just in fun.

Oh, you cra - zy moon, What did you do?
Oh, you cra - zy moon, Look what you've done.

44

THE ONE I LOVE

(BELONGS TO SOMEBODY ELSE)

Many people consider "The One I Love" to be one of the classiest songs of all. It was written by two of the most successful songwriters of the golden era of popular music. The lyricist, Gus Kahn, wrote the words for so many big hits — all the way from "Ain't We Got Fun?" to "You Stepped Out of a Dream" — that Hollywood later made a film about him, starring Danny Thomas as Gus and Doris Day as the girl he married. As musical biographies go, *I'll See You in My Dreams* was very well done. The film was named after one of Kahn's hits, which, like "The One I Love," has music composed by Isham Jones. In addition to being one of the best songsmiths of the time, Jones was also a popular bandleader.

Words by Gus Kahn; Music by Isham Jones

The one I love be-longs to some-bod-y else. _____ She

means her ten-der songs for some-bod-y else. _____ And

THE ONE I LOVE (BELONGS TO SOMEBODY ELSE)

48

Frank Sinatra recorded "Street of Dreams" on two occasions, 37 years apart. The first time was with Tommy Dorsey's orchestra in May 1942; the second was as part of his *Trilogy* LP in July 1979. In between, Frank sang a lot of lovely ballads, of course, but few as pretty and as simple as "Street of Dreams," which had been around for a number of years before Sinatra's first recording. It first saw the light of day in 1933, and like a lot of other songs of that period, it addresses itself directly to the Great Depression ("Poor, no one is poor, / Long as love is sure / On the Street of Dreams"). The ballad ranks right along with "In a Shanty in Old Shanty Town" and "Remember My Forgotten Man" as a reminder of the era of hard times.

Words by Sam M. Lewis; Music by Victor Young

STREET OF DREAMS

BLUE ORCHIDS

It's difficult to place Hoagy Carmichael in a comfortable niche. He wrote folksy songs; he wrote sophisticated songs. Sometimes he composed just the music; other times he wrote the lyrics as well. He wrote the most famous song of all, but even without "Star Dust," he ranks as one of the top dozen popular composers. And in mid-career he became a successful character actor in the movies, sort of playing . . . well . . . Hoagy Carmichael. This lovely song by Hoagy reached No. 1 on *Your Hit Parade* on November 4, 1939, thanks to Tommy Dorsey's beautiful and sensitive recording.

Words and Music by Hoagy Carmichael

I dreamed of two blue or-chids, Two beau-ti-ful blue or-chids, One night___ while in my lone-ly room. I dreamed of two blue or-chids So full of love and light That I want-ed to pos-sess each ten-der bloom. Then my dream took wings And through a thou-sand springs, Blue

SECTION THREE
GLENN MILLER AND BENNY GOODMAN HITS

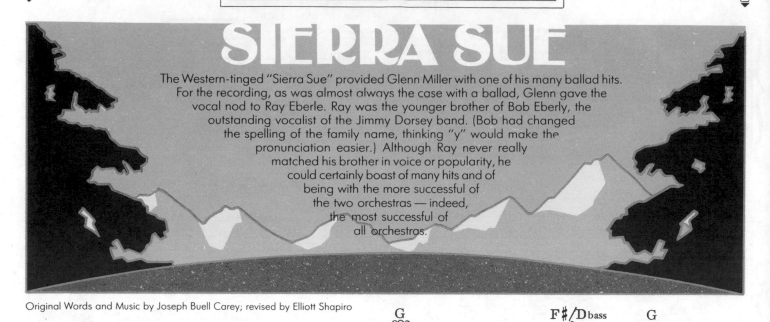

SIERRA SUE

The Western-tinged "Sierra Sue" provided Glenn Miller with one of his many ballad hits. For the recording, as was almost always the case with a ballad, Glenn gave the vocal nod to Ray Eberle. Ray was the younger brother of Bob Eberly, the outstanding vocalist of the Jimmy Dorsey band. (Bob had changed the spelling of the family name, thinking "y" would make the pronunciation easier.) Although Ray never really matched his brother in voice or popularity, he could certainly boast of many hits and of being with the more successful of the two orchestras — indeed, the most successful of all orchestras.

Original Words and Music by Joseph Buell Carey; revised by Elliott Shapiro

ELMER'S TUNE

Words and Music by Elmer Albrecht, Sammy Gallop and Dick Jurgens

Lilting swing

Why are the stars al - ways wink-in' and blink-in' a - bove? What makes a
la - dy of eight-y go out on the loose? Why does a

fel - low start think-in' of fall - in' in love? It's not the sea-son, the rea-son is
gan-der me - an - der in search of a goose? What puts the kick in a chick-en, the

1.
plain as the moon;___ It's just El - mer's Tune. What makes a
mag - ic in June?___

2.
It's just El - mer's Tune. Lis - ten,___ Lis - ten,___

56

It was at the famed Aragon Ballroom in Chicago that this song came into being by way of one of the top midwestern orchestras, led by Dick Jurgens and featuring vocalist Eddy Howard. A neighbor and regular at the Aragon was a fellow named Elmer Albrecht. Well, Elmer just happened to have a tune, which he brought to Dick, and you know the rest. But guess what? The Jurgens band didn't have the big hit with the song. Glenn Miller and His Orchestra did. As a matter of fact, with its stellar vocal by Ray Eberle and The Modernaires, the recording of "Elmer's Tune" became one of Miller's biggest hits ever, attesting once again to the enormous popularity of the band.

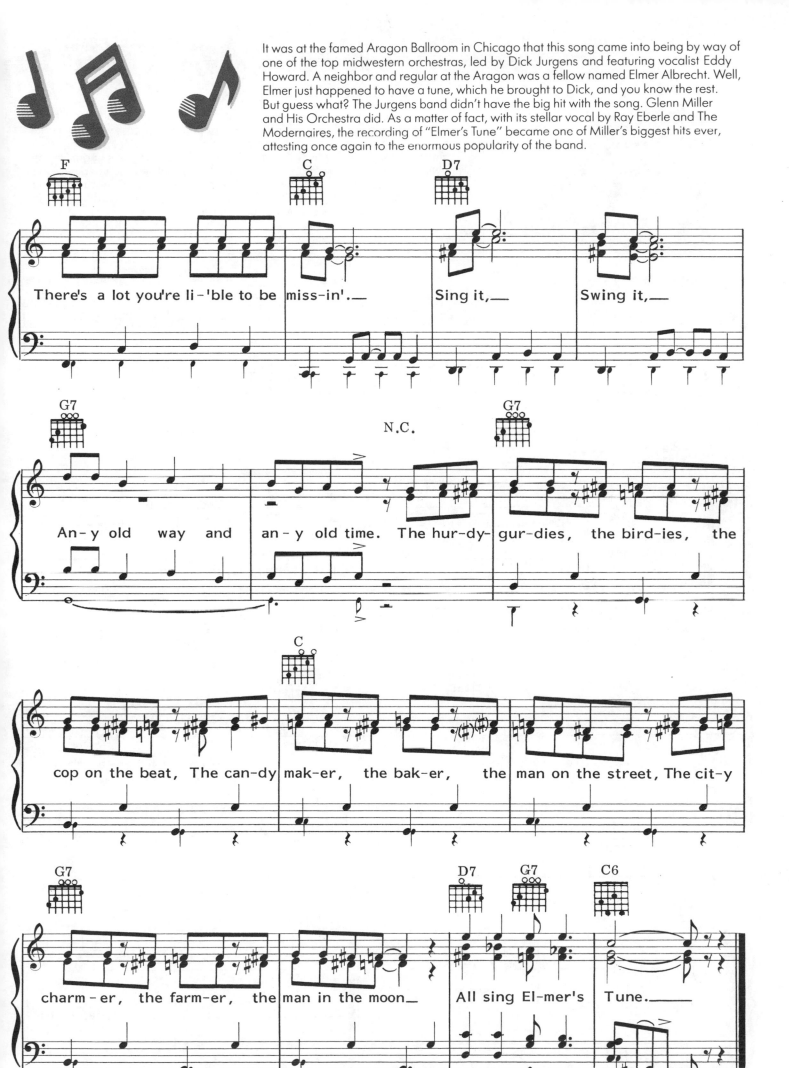

There's a lot you're li-'ble to be miss-in'. Sing it, Swing it, An-y old way and an-y old time. The hur-dy-gur-dies, the bird-ies, the cop on the beat, The can-dy mak-er, the bak-er, the man on the street, The cit-y charm-er, the farm-er, the man in the moon All sing El-mer's Tune.

57

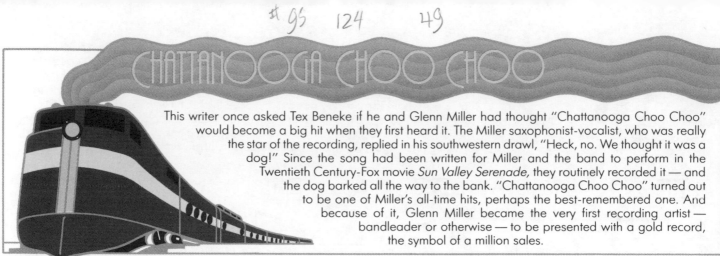

CHATTANOOGA CHOO CHOO

This writer once asked Tex Beneke if he and Glenn Miller had thought "Chattanooga Choo Choo" would become a big hit when they first heard it. The Miller saxophonist-vocalist, who was really the star of the recording, replied in his southwestern drawl, "Heck, no. We thought it was a dog!" Since the song had been written for Miller and the band to perform in the Twentieth Century-Fox movie *Sun Valley Serenade*, they routinely recorded it — and the dog barked all the way to the bank. "Chattanooga Choo Choo" turned out to be one of Miller's all-time hits, perhaps the best-remembered one. And because of it, Glenn Miller became the very first recording artist — bandleader or otherwise — to be presented with a gold record, the symbol of a million sales.

From *Sun Valley Serenade*
Words by Mack Gordon; Music by Harry Warren

61

SUNRISE SERENADE

Glenn Miller's popularity was such that he had several hits with songs that originated with other bands. As we've noted earlier, "Elmer's Tune" was first played by Dick Jurgens, and "Tuxedo Junction" had its start with Erskine Hawkins, but both songs became internationally prominent via Miller waxings. Another prime example was "Sunrise Serenade," written by the piano player in the Horace Heidt orchestra, a genial fellow named Frankie Carle, who would later lead his own big band and rack up hit records. The veteran lyricist Jack Lawrence later added words to Carle's tune, but the song's big success came with Glenn Miller's instrumental version. "Sunrise Serenade" appeared on a 1939 recording. The flip side of that record was to be the maestro's as-yet-untitled theme song. To complement the "sunrise" part of the recording, Miller asked Mitchell Parish to write some "evening" lyrics for his theme. And that's how "Moonlight Serenade" got its name.

Words by Jack Lawrence; Music by Frankie Carle

Good morn-in', Good morn-in', You sleep-y-head. It's dawn-in', Stop yawn-in', Get out of that bed. Say the air is soft as silk; It's time to get the morn-in' milk. Come on!

"Stairway to the Stars" was yet another Glenn Miller hit, and an early one. The lyrics were written by the incomparable Mitchell Parish, whose specialty was taking a song that had already appeared as an instrumental piece and adding words to it — "Star Dust," "Sophisticated Lady," "Don't Be That Way." Indeed, as we've seen, he put lyrics to Glenn Miller's theme and thereby helped establish "Moonlight Serenade" as an important standard. Parish once told this writer that Paul Whiteman, long after he had commissioned George Gershwin to write "Rhapsody in Blue," continued to authorize other "serious" (or concert) works. One of them was "Park Avenue Fantasy," written by the band's pianist, Frank Signorelli, and one of the violinists, Matty Malneck. With Parish's perfect lyrics, a portion of the "Fantasy" became the lovely "Stairway to the Stars."

STAIRWAY TO THE STARS

Words by Mitchell Parish; Music by Matty Malneck and Frank Signorelli

There's a sil-ver trail of moon-light Lead-ing up-ward to the sky, And the night is like a vel-vet lull-a-by. There's a heav-en of blue, And we'll go there just you and I.

Please Be Kind

The Benny Goodman band, which led all others into the Big Band Era in 1935, was known primarily for its great rollicking tunes — "Sing, Sing, Sing," "Don't Be That Way," "Goody-Goody" and "Bob White," to name a few. However, the robust, talented organization could also mount a pretty ballad, doing several with a little lilting beat — as it did with "Please Be Kind." The song was written by Saul Chaplin and Sammy Cahn, a team that had had a remarkable success a short time before with an adaptation of a Yiddish song called "Bei Mir Bist Du Schön." Both gentlemen would go on to enjoy tremendous careers in Hollywood. Chaplin became a major force in film studios as arranger-songwriter-head of department, particularly at Columbia. And Cahn, in tandem with Jule Styne and later with Jimmy Van Heusen, became one of the two or three most prolific and successful lyricists in movie history.

Words and Music by Sammy Cahn and Saul Chaplin

Slowly and somewhat freely

This is my first af-fair, So please be kind.

Han-dle my heart with care, Oh, please be kind.

This is all so grand; My dreams are on pa-rade. If

69

D7
Dm7
Fm6
F/G
G7 6
you'll just un - der - stand, They'll nev - er, nev - er fade. So
F♯m7-5
F9
Em7
E♭dim
Dm7
A♭9
G7 6
8va
tell me your love's sin - cere, Oh, please be kind.
Gm7
G♭9
F6 9
Tell me I need - n't fear, Oh, please be kind. 'Cause
Fm7
Fm6
Em7
A7
A♭7
A7
if you leave me, dear, I know my heart will lose its mind. If you
D9
Fm6
F/G
No chords
Cmaj9
love me, Please be kind.

IT'S BEEN SO LONG

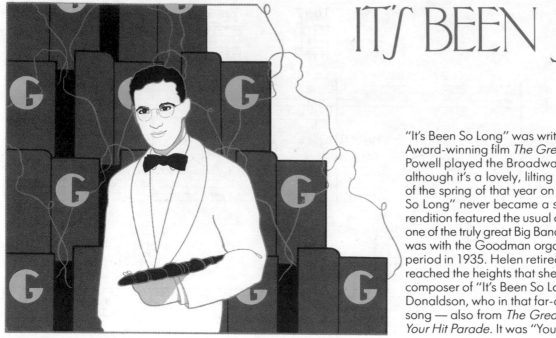

"It's Been So Long" was written for the 1936 Academy Award-winning film *The Great Ziegfeld,* in which William Powell played the Broadway impresario. Curiously, although it's a lovely, lilting affair and lingered for most of the spring of that year on *Your Hit Parade,* "It's Been So Long" never became a standard. Benny Goodman's rendition featured the usual clarinet solo and a neat vocal by one of the truly great Big Band Era vocalists, Helen Ward, who was with the Goodman organization during its breakthrough period in 1935. Helen retired early and consequently never reached the heights that she might have otherwise. The composer of "It's Been So Long" was the fabled Walter Donaldson, who in that far-off spring of 1936 had another song — also from *The Great Ziegfeld* — reach No. 1 on *Your Hit Parade.* It was "You," the theme of the movie.

Words and Music by Harold Adamson and Walter Donaldson

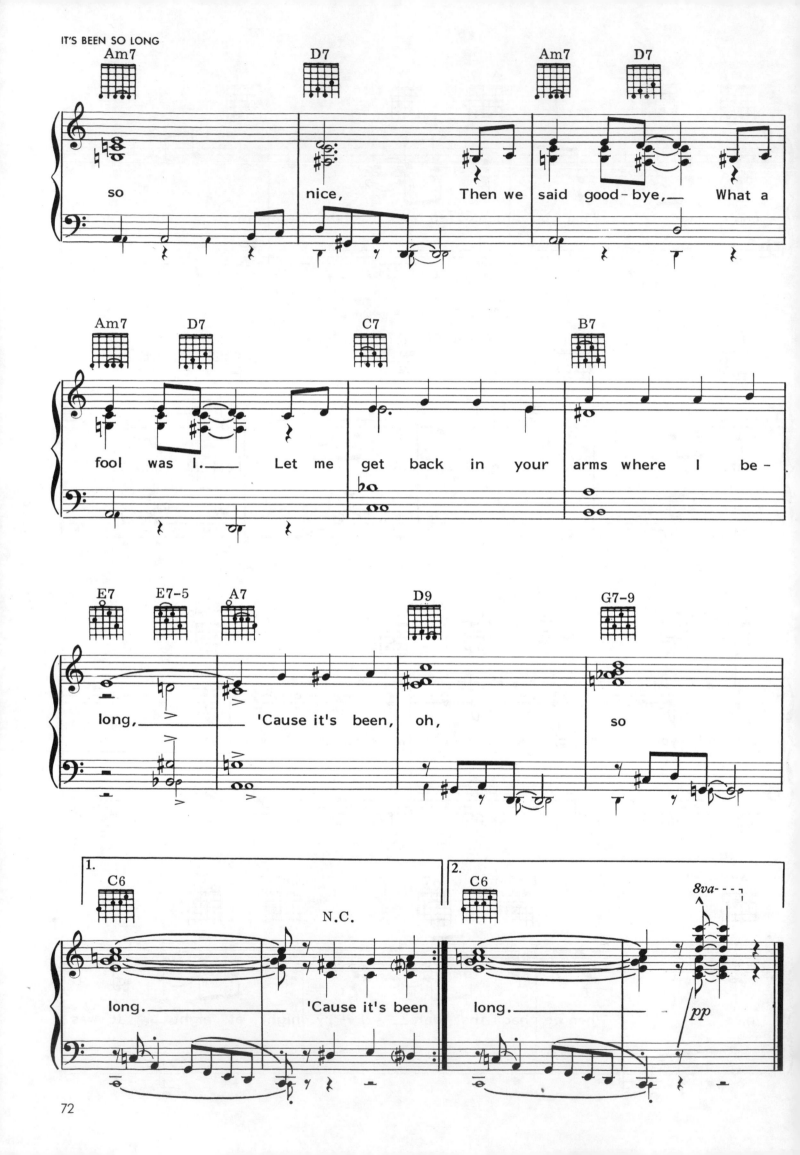

And the angels sing

This song originated with the great Benny Goodman band. Johnny Mercer, in the early days of his brilliant and multifaceted career, appeared with Goodman on a radio series called *Camel Caravan*. Among the standout musicians in Benny's group was the trumpet star Ziggy Elman, who numbered among his featured solos something he had dubbed "Fralich in Swing." The tune, based on a Yiddish folk song, caught Mercer's fancy. He added words to it, and, as "And the Angels Sing," it became another hit for the Goodman band when they recorded it with "Liltin' " Martha Tilton on the vocal. Incidentally, "And the Angels Sing" had such staying power that some years later, in 1944, Paramount gave that title to a musical starring Betty Hutton, and the movie in turn helped to sustain the song, which is still loved today.

Words by Johnny Mercer; Music by Ziggy Elman

This song was by no means Benny Goodman's first hit, but it was the first for a lady who has had many since and who went on to become one of the premiere artists of our time. Peggy Lee was singing in a Chicago cocktail lounge when Benny first heard her in 1941. It so happened that Helen Forrest had just left Goodman in favor of Harry James, so Benny hired Miss Lee as his new vocalist. With Goodman, Peggy electrified America with "Why Don't You Do Right." The original recording of the song had been done in a much slower, bluesier tempo and idiom by a black Chicago singer named Lil Green. But the Lee-Goodman version is a classic example of a song finding exactly the right singer and band —and what a band! Many musicologists rate Goodman's 1941–42 band, with those memorable Eddie Sauter arrangements, as his finest.

WHY DON'T YOU DO RIGHT

Words and Music by Joe McCoy

* Lil Green and Peggy Lee sang "wim-men."

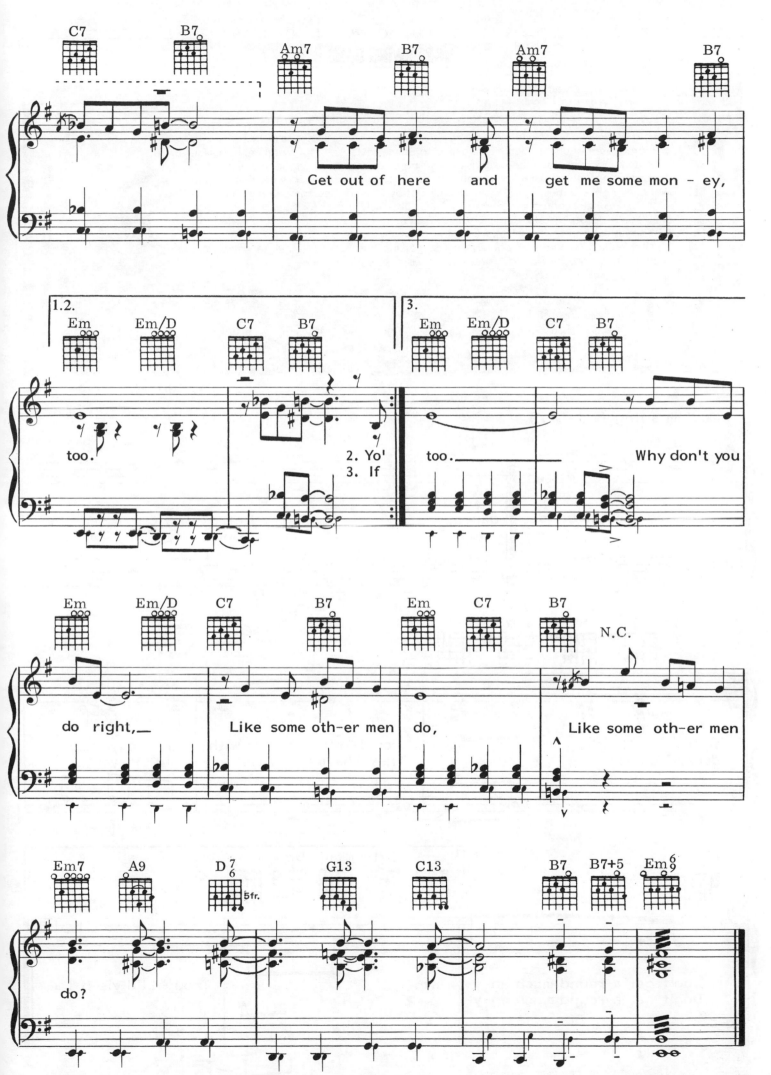

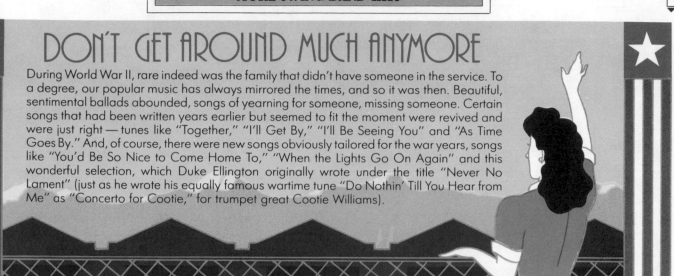

DON'T GET AROUND MUCH ANYMORE

During World War II, rare indeed was the family that didn't have someone in the service. To a degree, our popular music has always mirrored the times, and so it was then. Beautiful, sentimental ballads abounded, songs of yearning for someone, missing someone. Certain songs that had been written years earlier but seemed to fit the moment were revived and were just right — tunes like "Together," "I'll Get By," "I'll Be Seeing You" and "As Time Goes By." And, of course, there were new songs obviously tailored for the war years, songs like "You'd Be So Nice to Come Home To," "When the Lights Go On Again" and this wonderful selection, which Duke Ellington originally wrote under the title "Never No Lament" (just as he wrote his equally famous wartime tune "Do Nothin' Till You Hear from Me" as "Concerto for Cootie," for trumpet great Cootie Williams).

Words by Bob Russell; Music by Duke Ellington

Missed the Sat-ur-day dance,
club,
Heard they crowd-ed the
Got as far as the

floor,
door;
Could-n't bear it with-out you,___
They'd have asked me a-bout you,___

Don't get a-round much an-y-more.
Don't get a-round much an-y-
Thought I'd vis-it the

DEEP IN A DREAM

"My cigarette burns me, I wake with a start. My hand isn't hurt, but there's pain in my heart." Today, fewer and fewer people are smoking. But back when this song was written — in 1938 — nearly everybody did. Popular music reflected the fact. Camel cigarettes sponsored Benny Goodman on *The Camel Caravan;* Glenn Miller worked for Chesterfield; Lucky Strike presented *Your Hit Parade* for more than two decades; Philip Morris had Russ Morgan; and Artie Shaw was on the air under the aegis of Old Gold. And the tobacco connection went beyond mere sponsorship — the songs themselves had the habit. Think of "Two Cigarettes in the Dark," "While a Cigarette Was Burning" and "Smoke Rings," and you begin to get the cloudy idea.

Words by Eddie De Lange; Music by Jimmy Van Heusen

I Don't Want to Walk Without You

Just as some of the greatest Broadway songs came from flop shows that lasted only a couple of weeks, some of the biggest Hollywood tunes came from "B" films, or "programmers," as they were called, their purpose being to flesh out a double bill. In fact, in the time it used to take to sit through the standard two feature films, plus the two-reel comedy, the newsreel and previews of coming attractions, today one could fly from New York to Los Angeles. This great song was from a typical "B" movie, a little beaut called *Sweater Girl*. Although the picture was a low-budget quickie, "I Don't Want to Walk Without You" was written by two of the greatest popular songwriters ever, Frank Loesser and Jule Styne. The magnificent Harry James – Helen Forrest hit recording of it is still a staple on big-band radio stations today.

Words by Frank Loesser; Music by Jule Styne

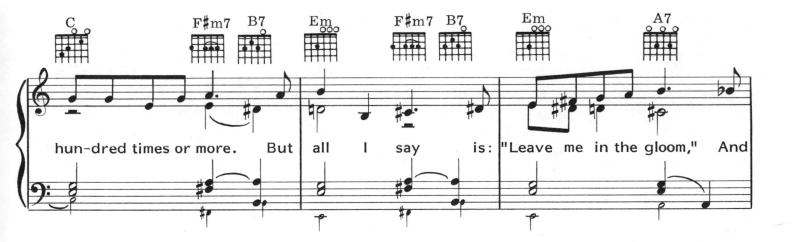

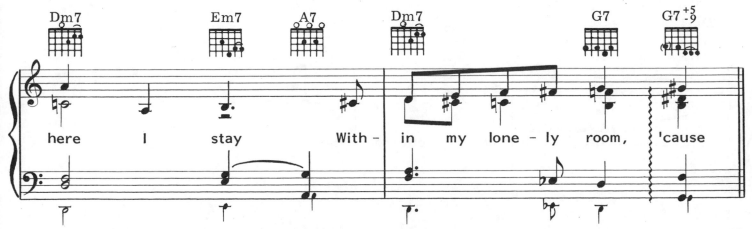

I HAD THE CRAZIEST DREAM

During World War II, the popularity of big bands was so great that such orchestras as those of Glenn Miller, Artie Shaw, Benny Goodman, Sammy Kaye and both the Dorsey brothers were being featured in motion pictures on a regular basis. By 1942, after his big breakthrough with "You Made Me Love You," Hollywood called for Harry James. Twentieth Century-Fox placed him in a movie entitled *Springtime in the Rockies,* which featured Betty Grable, whom he eventually married. In the film, however, and on the subsequent best-selling recording, it was James' great vocalist Helen Forrest who sang "I Had the Craziest Dream."

Words by Mack Gordon; Music by Harry Warren

President Franklin D. Roosevelt's Good Neighbor Policy toward Latin America certainly had the backing of Tin Pan Alley — Latin American songs were sweeping the country at the time. There were several reasons for the phenomenon. First was ASCAP's (American Society of Composers, Authors and Publishers) decision, in 1941, to forbid songs under its aegis from being played on the radio. This meant that foreign songs like "Maria Elena," "Amapola," "Green Eyes" and "Yours" were in great demand and became hits. Second, those songs, plus "The Breeze and I," were all Jimmy Dorsey hits, usually with vocals by Bob Eberly and Helen O'Connell. (Bob soloed on "Maria Elena.") And third, the Americas, both North and South, were at peace, so a certain amount of escapism may have been at work. In any case, all these songs and more were on the Top 10 list for some time. And, of course, there were ersatz Latin airs like "South America, Take It Away," "Tangerine" and "Six Lessons from Madame La Zonga" (just to keep things dishonest).

MARIA ELENA

English words by S.K. Russell;
Spanish words and music by Lorenzo Barcelata

Waltz tempo-rather freely

Ma – ri –a E–le – na, You're the an–swer to a pray'r. Ma – ri –a E–le–na,
Tu-yo es mi co-ra– zón Oh sol de mi que– rer. Mu-jer de mi i-lu-

Can't you see how much I care? To me your voice is
sión, Mi a-mor te con sa– gré. Mi vi – da la em-be-

like the ech–o of a sigh, And when you're near my heart can't speak a–
lle –ce u-na es-pe-ran– za a–zul, Mi vi – da tie-ne un cie – lo que le

FRENESÍ

In 1939, Artie Shaw walked away from his band (walked right off the bandstand, in fact) at the height of its popularity and took off for Mexico. There, he discovered a couple of tunes that he soon brought back to the United States, his fiesta-siesta having been short-lived. Instead of returning to New York, Artie went to Los Angeles. So eager was he to record the Latin songs that he did the date with a Hollywood "pickup" band, consisting of musicians working around town. One song was called "Adiós, Mariquita Linda," and the other was "Frenesí." America waved *adiós* to Mariquita Linda but said *buenos días* in a big way to "Frenesí." The song hit the charts in December 1940 and stayed in the Top 10 (in first place for three straight weeks) until mid-April of 1941. Whether he liked it or not, Artie Shaw was back in the music business again.

English words by Ray Charles and S.K. Russell; Spanish words and music by Alberto Dominguez

Moderate Latin feel

Some time_ a-go
Bé-sa-me tú a mí

I wan-dered down in-to old Mex-i-co.
Bé-sa-me igual que mi bo-ca te be-só

While I___ was there,
Da-me el fre-ne-sí

I felt ro-mance ev-'ry-
Que mi lo-cu-ra te

where.___
dió.___

Moon was shin-ing bright,
Quien si no fuí yo

And I could hear laugh-ing
Pu-do en-se-ñar-te el ca-

I HEAR A RHAPSODY

Words and Music by George Fragos, Jack Baker and Dick Gasparre

Hit songs are funny things. Take, for example, "I Hear a Rhapsody." A lovely, exotic melody with exciting lyrics, it was in the Top 10 for 15 straight weeks. ("White Christmas" would tie for that honor a year later.) Today, "I Hear a Rhapsody" is no longer a major standard, but it's still a beautiful, haunting song, a dark and brooding minor melody. One of its writers, Dick Gasparre, had his own band, but more people would probably connect the song to saxophonist-bandleader Charlie Barnet because of his 1941 hit recording.

I LET A SONG GO OUT OF MY HEART

Words by Irving Mills, Henry Nemo and John Redmond;
Music by Duke Ellington

Much has been written about the 1930s being the golden age of American popular music. There were, in retrospect, several reasons for this. Besides the relentless and wonderful onslaught of Hollywood musicals — good, bad or indifferent, but all requiring big songs, many of them written by the giants of Broadway — there were the big bands. In addition, network radio devoted hours each week to "band remotes" — pickups of orchestras from hotels, cafés and ballrooms throughout the United States. Some of the great 1930s songs came directly from the bands. "I Let a Song Go Out of My Heart," for example, was wafted out of the Duke Ellington organization — Duke wrote it himself — and made it to the Top 10 and finally to No. 1 in the summer of 1938. It's a beauty.

Nice and easy

I let a song— go out of my heart; It was the sweet-est
Since you and I___ have drift-ed a-part, Life does-n't mean a

mel - o - dy.___ I know I___ lost heav - en___ 'Cause
thing to me.___ Please come back,_ sweet mu - sic, I

you were the song.
know I was wrong.

Am I too late___

To make a - mends?___ You know that we were meant to

SO RARE

The 1930s were great years for American popular music. It would be, in fact, almost impossible to list all the hits of that decade. But for the record, just look at 1937 alone, in terms of songs that are standards, songs that you still hear today. Some of the biggest hits of that year were: "It's De-Lovely," "I've Got You Under My Skin," "Pennies from Heaven," "The Way You Look Tonight," "Easy to Love," "Good Night, My Love," "Too Marvelous for Words," "Where Are You?," "September in the Rain," "There's a Lull in My Life," "Let's Call the Whole Thing Off," "They Can't Take That Away from Me," "Blue Hawaii," "A Sailboat in the Moonlight," "Where or When," "That Old Feeling," "Harbor Lights" and "Nice Work If You Can Get It." Oh, yes, and this song, "So Rare," which enjoyed a big revival as a Jimmy Dorsey recording 20 years later. One can only wonder how many songs from the 1980s will be remembered half a century from now.

Words by Jack Sharpe; Music by Jerry Herst

"Rose O'Day" was one of the many hits played by Sammy Kaye, the old Swing and Sway maestro. Sammy started his first band in Athens, Ohio, while studying engineering at Ohio University. He and his band later became a hotel staple in New York, introducing songs by singing out their titles, and for many years Sammy had a popular Sunday network radio program on which he read poetry. One of this writer's fondest

ROSE O'DAY

(THE FILLA-GA-DUSHA SONG)

memories of Sammy Kaye goes back to a time not long before his death in 1987. I was emceeing a jazz music affair at Eddie Condon's in New York. Now, Sammy would have been the first to tell you that he was a very pedestrian clarinetist. In introducing the various celebrities in attendance, I acknowledged Benny Goodman, and one of the spectators yelled, "Play, Benny!" To which Sammy declared, "He's embarrassed to play in front of me."

Words and Music by Charles Tobias and Al Lewis

THERE GOES THAT SONG AGAIN

You could list this one under the heading "nothing exceeds like success." A couple of years before penning this tune, Sammy Cahn and Jule Styne had hit pay dirt with the first song they wrote together. It was called "I've Heard That Song Before," and thanks to a big, splashy hit record by Harry James and Helen Forrest, it had a life-span in the Top 10 of an astounding 15 straight weeks during the winter and spring of 1943. By the summer of that wartime year, nearly everybody had "heard that song before." Thus armed with success, Sammy and Jule decided to revisit the well and found that there was still water in it. Although it failed to enjoy quite the experience of its kissing cousin, "There Goes That Song Again" was No. 2 for five straight weeks in early 1945.

Words by Sammy Cahn; Music by Jule Styne

Words by Bill Carey; Music by Carl Fischer

One important asset of big-band leaders was their emceeing ability, which varied greatly. Tommy Dorsey was a better emcee than his brother Jimmy. Woody Herman was very good, and Glenn Miller was effective in a straight-arrow way. Benny Goodman was leaden; Guy Lombardo, excellent. Perhaps the best of the bunch was Kay Kyser. In fact, Kay later became a principal figure in radio and early television, emceeing *Kay Kyser's Kollege of Musical Knowledge,* one of the era's top audience-participation shows. Kay and his orchestra had struggled for several years before hitting on the Kollege idea and their vocalizations of song introductions. Kyser then rode to fame and fortune, while always playing very danceable music and occasionally, as was the case with "Who Wouldn't Love You," scoring with a big hit record.

A Sailboat in the Moonlight

If ever there was a family affair in the music business, it was Guy Lombardo and His Royal Canadians. In addition to Guy, there were brothers Carmen, Victor and Lebert — all continuously with the band except for a brief time when Victor went out on his own — sister Rosemarie, who sang with the band for a short while, and Kenny Gardner, who more or less succeeded Carmen as vocalist and was married to another sister, Elaine. Carmen Lombardo, in addition to playing saxophone in the band and being its star vocalist for a long time, was the musical director of the organization. But Carmen was something else, too. He was one of the more successful songwriters of the era, with such big hits as "Sweethearts on Parade," "Snuggled on Your Shoulder," "Seems Like Old Times," "Boo-Hoo!" and this lovely lilting melody, which he sang on the band's hit recording. Carmen had a very fluctuating, breathy but sincere voice, which sounded, in a strange way, like the saxophone section of the band.

Words and Music by Carmen Lombardo and John Jacob Loeb

Moderately slow, in 2 (♩ = 1 beat)

sail-boat in the moon-light and you;___ Would-n't that be

heav - en, A heav - en just for two?

soft breeze on a June night and you;___ What a per-fect

TONIGHT We Love

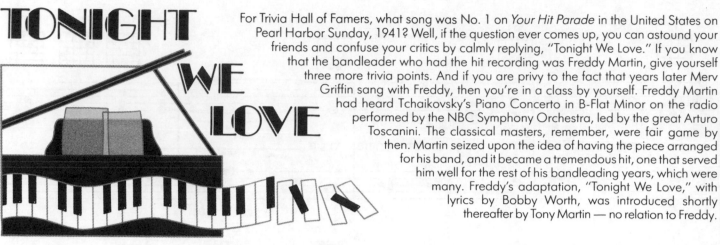

For Trivia Hall of Famers, what song was No. 1 on *Your Hit Parade* in the United States on Pearl Harbor Sunday, 1941? Well, if the question ever comes up, you can astound your friends and confuse your critics by calmly replying, "Tonight We Love." If you know that the bandleader who had the hit recording was Freddy Martin, give yourself three more trivia points. And if you are privy to the fact that years later Merv Griffin sang with Freddy, then you're in a class by yourself. Freddy Martin had heard Tchaikovsky's Piano Concerto in B-Flat Minor on the radio performed by the NBC Symphony Orchestra, led by the great Arturo Toscanini. The classical masters, remember, were fair game by then. Martin seized upon the idea of having the piece arranged for his band, and it became a tremendous hit, one that served him well for the rest of his bandleading years, which were many. Freddy's adaptation, "Tonight We Love," with lyrics by Bobby Worth, was introduced shortly thereafter by Tony Martin — no relation to Freddy.

Words by Bobby Worth; Music adapted by Ray Austin and Freddy Martin from Tchaikovsky's Concerto in B-Flat Minor

ours._____ Night winds that sigh Em-brace the sky._____

_____ To-night we love in the glow_____ That gleams so

soft - ly I know._____ This was - n't

MY REVERIE

Although it did not go on to establish itself as one of the major standards, the beautiful "My Reverie" broke into the charts like a bolt from the blue in 1938, reaching No. 1 in August and staying there for almost two months. It was written and made a hit by Larry Clinton, a top bandleader of the period, who is, however, not as well remembered as the Dorseys, Glenn Miller, Artie Shaw, Benny Goodman and others. Nicknamed The Dipsy Doodler after one of his compositions (made famous by Tommy Dorsey's band), Clinton was a noted arranger and composer as well as bandleader. He based "My Reverie" on Claude Debussy's lovely "Reverie." Not only was it the first adaptation of a piece of classical music to gain top popularity, it opened the floodgates for the future Tchaikovsky- and Rachmaninoff-based "adaptations," including "Our Love" from Tchaikovsky's *Romeo and Juliet Overture-Fantasy*.

Words and Music by Larry Clinton

Moderately slow

pp -- soft and dreamy

Our love ___ Is a dream, but in my rev-er-ie, ___ I can see that this love was meant ___ for me. On-ly a

SCATTERBRAIN

In his revised edition of *The Big Bands,* musicologist George T. Simon does full biographical sketches on 72 of the best-known bands and their leaders and briefer rundowns on more than 200 others. Among the latter group of bandleaders is a fellow named Frankie Masters. Seemingly, for those nearly 300 bands, there was a hotel for each to play in, from the Astor in New York to the Muehlebach in Kansas City, from the Ambassador in Los Angeles to the Chase

in St. Louis. For Frankie Masters, home base for a good deal of his career was the Taft Hotel in New York City and the Stevens (later the Conrad Hilton) in Chicago. And for every band or band-leader, there was a signature theme. Frankie's was "Scatterbrain," one of his own compositions. An astonishing number of those lesser-known bands at one time or another had a hit, and Frankie Masters' was no exception. His "Scatterbrain" theme made it all the way to No. 1.

Words by Johnny Burke; Music by Khan Keene, Carl Bean and Frankie Masters

With a lilt (♩♪ = ♪³♪) (like a schottische)

You're as | pleas-ant as the morn-ing and re- | fresh-ing as the rain;
(You're as) | gay as New Year par-ties; you're as | sweet as su-gar-cane,

Is -n't it a pit - y that you're | such a scat-ter-brain? When you
But when you get ser - i - ous, you're | such a scat-ter-brain. When we

smile it's so de - light-ful, When you | talk it's so in - sane;
dance I think it's heav-en Till a - | bout the third re - frain;

Still it's charm-ing chat-ter, scat-ter-brain. I know I'll end up ap-o-plec-tic, But there's
Then you start your pat-ter, scat-ter-brain. Per-haps I'm much too an-a-lyt - ic, But I'm

noth - ing I can do; It's just the same as be - ing in a hur - ri -
up the well-known tree; I've tried to un - der-stand your dou - ble-talk in

cane. And though my life will be too hec - tic, I'm so
vain. Yet won't you please for - give your crit - ic 'Cause you

much in love with you; Noth - ing else can mat - ter; You're my
mean so much to me; Noth - ing else can mat - ter; You're my

1.
dar - ling scat - ter - brain. You're as

2.
dar - ling scat - ter - brain.

Words and Music by Billy Hill

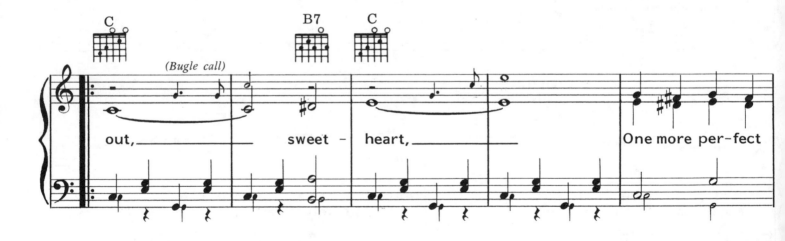

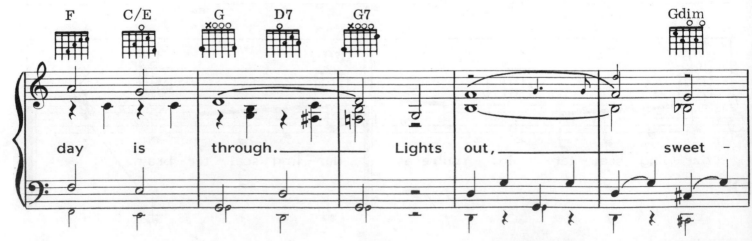

Like so many other ballads and novelty songs of the middle part of this century, "Lights Out" was nurtured by Guy Lombardo and His Royal Canadians. It was written by a man from Boston named William J. (Billy) Hill. His sojourn in the West — working with surveyors in Death Valley and leading a band in Salt Lake City — seems to have had a remarkable, and profitable, influence on his songwriting. Within a period of three or four years, he had

three tremendous hits with a definite Western accent. "Wagon Wheels," "Empty Saddles" and "The Last Round-Up" may have been ersatz cowboy, but they certainly were chart-busters. "Lights Out," though not in that genre, has the same down-home appeal and feeling of built-in nostalgia and, like those other songs, was a big hit. Thanks to a recording by pianist Eddy Duchin, the song reached No. 1 on *Your Hit Parade* early in 1936.

YOU'RE BREAKING MY HEART

As is also true of the word "moon," without the word "heart" there would have been no Tin Pan Alley. It was, well, the music industry's "Heart and Soul" (which, by the way, is the first of more than 100 songs in the ASCAP Index that *start* with the word "heart"). The good Lord only knows how many other songs include the heart somewhere in their titles or lyrics. Of course, there are so many things you can do with a heart. You can endow it with inane qualities ("My Foolish Heart"), dress it ("My Heart's Wrapped Up in Gingham"), seek divine guidance for it ("Heaven Help This Heart of Mine"), donate it ("My Heart Belongs to Daddy"), take it out on the town ("My Heart Is Dancing"), send it on the road ("My Heart Is a Hobo"), put it on the telephone ("My Heart Is Calling"), read it ("My Heart Is an Open Book"), suspend it ("My Heart Stood Still") or cause it pain (there are at least five songs called "Heartaches"). And, of course, everybody knows that "You've Gotta Have Heart." For the record, "You're Breaking My Heart," set to "Mattinata," a melody by Italian opera composer Ruggiero Leoncavallo *(Pagliacci),* became a hit via a recording by that outstanding Italian-American singer Vic Damone.

Words and Music by Pat Genaro and Sunny Skylar

THE THINGS WE DID LAST SUMMER

In 1946, "The Things We Did Last Summer" joined the long, steady stream of hits by the wonderful Jo Stafford, a Tommy Dorsey alumna and one of the classiest and most talented vocalists of her era. As a matter of fact, Jo had a bunch of hits in 1946–47. In addition to this one, there were "Symphony," "You Keep Coming Back Like a Song" and "Feudin' and Fightin'." Before her Dorsey days, she had been part of a country-oriented group called The Stafford Singers in Los Angeles, right next door to her hometown of Long Beach. Joining Tommy as a member of the fabled vocal group The Pied Pipers, she got the classic big-band training that would serve her so well when she went out on her own during the war. Jo's hits continued well into the 1950s with such stunning successes as "You Belong to Me" and "Jambalaya."

Words by Sammy Cahn; Music by Jule Styne

Chord symbols are a somewhat simplified version of piano part.

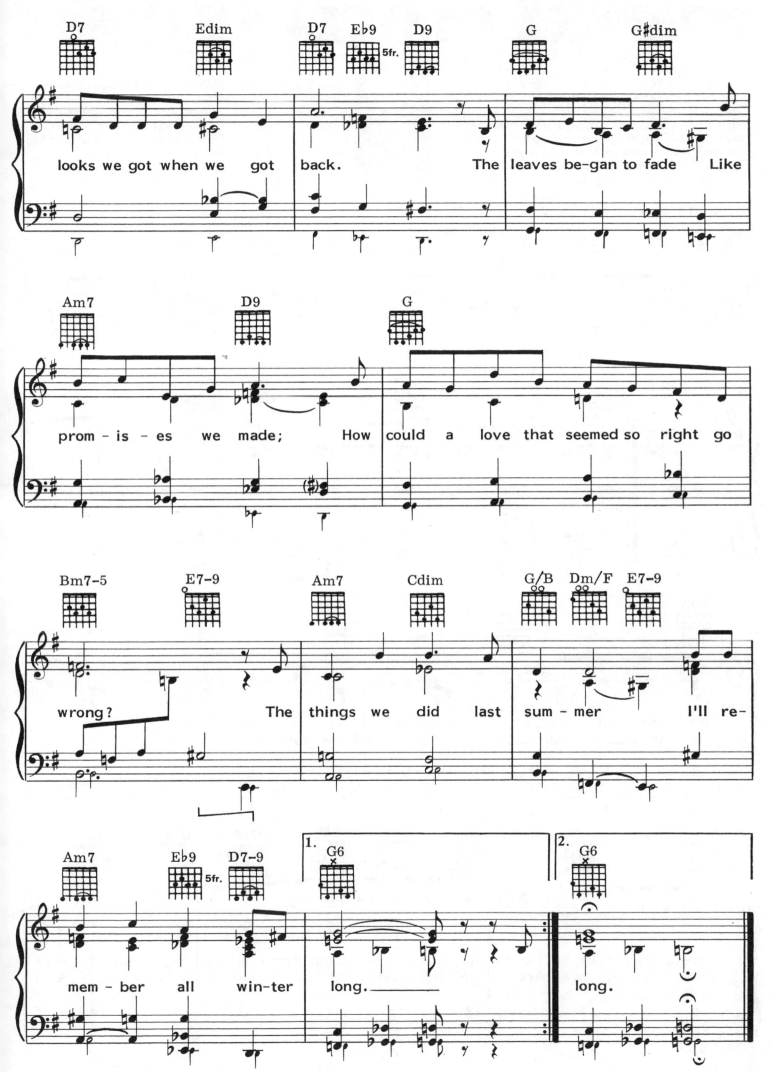

looks we got when we got back. The leaves be-gan to fade Like

prom - is - es we made; How could a love that seemed so right go

wrong? The things we did last sum - mer I'll re-

mem - ber all win - ter long. long.

DO I WORRY

Like "Ballerina" (see page 136), "Do I Worry?" is a song that was big enough to support two hit records in 1941, one by The Ink Spots, the other by Tommy Dorsey and His Orchestra with Frank Sinatra on the vocal. The Ink Spots, Dorsey and Sinatra, of course, were all hit-laden through the rest of the decade. The United States did not enter World War II until late that year, but there was a battle — a musical one — going on at home. Since the American Society of Composers, Authors and Publishers (ASCAP), the organization that controlled practically all popular music, had pulled its songs off the airwaves, it was inevitable that a vacuum would develop. The fledgling Broadcast Music, Inc. (BMI), set up by the radio networks, rushed to fill the gap with its own songs, some of them quite good, thus allaying fears that *Your Hit Parade* would be dominated by tunes that were in the public domain, tunes like the Stephen Foster classics "I Dream of Jeanie" and "Beautiful Dreamer." "Do I Worry?" was one of BMI's songs that rushed to the *Hit Parade* and stayed there for three straight months in 1941.

Words and Music by Bobby Worth and Stanley Cowan

#61   92   49

Amor

Half of the songs of the 1940s were played and sung against the backdrop of World War II. This period coincided not only with the invasion of North Africa and Europe by the Allies but also with the invasion of North America by songs from Latin America. Some were hot, some languid and some, like "Amor," were sort of on the border, ballads with a Latin beat. "Amor" was one of the most popular and long-lasting songs of the period. Andy Russell had a best-selling recording of it in 1944, and the song was on *Your Hit Parade* from late May until October. It was No. 1 only twice, and strangely enough those two top-slot appearances were nearly a month apart.

English words by Sunny Skylar; Spanish words by Ricardo Lopez Mendez; Music by Gabriel Ruiz

You Can't Be True, Dear

Although "You Can't Be True, Dear" was a big vocal hit for Jerry Wayne, it was organist Ken Griffin's accompaniment on the recording that made the song the biggest thing to hit the ice- and roller-skating rinks since "The Skaters Waltz." "You Can't Be True, Dear" was, in a word, schmaltzy, no two ways about that. Some might even go so far as to label it corny, but be that as it may, it was a big song — in the Top 10 for parts of three seasons, the spring, summer and fall of 1948. In spite of the fact that three other songs — "Now Is the Hour," "A Tree in the Meadow" and "Buttons and Bows" — were collectively No. 1 for an astounding 30 weeks that year, "You Can't Be True, Dear" managed to sneak into the top spot for three weeks, a far piece from Germany, where, as "Du Kannst Nicht Treu Sein," the song first saw the light of day. Lyricist Hal Cotton was actually Dave Dreyer, who wrote such tunes as "Me and My Shadow," "Cecilia," "Back in Your Own Back Yard" and "There's a Rainbow 'Round My Shoulder."

English words by Hal Cotton; German words by Gerhard Ebeler;
Music by Hans Otten and Ken Griffin

Slow waltz tempo

Note: R.H. to be played 8va higher throughout

Mam'selle

This is one of the loveliest songs of the 1940s. It was written originally as background music for *The Razor's Edge,* which starred Tyrone Power, Gene Tierney and Anne Baxter. The melody, composed by the film's director, Edmund Goulding, proved so popular that Twentieth Century-Fox called in Mack Gordon, its ace lyricist, to add words. It was a wise move: "Mam'selle" became one of the major song successes in the years following World War II. The hit record was by a very fine singer named Art Lund, who unfortunately did not have many hits. Lund had previously been with Benny Goodman for a time, during which he used the name Art London. Some years later he found his niche on Broadway as one of the stars of Frank Loesser's *The Most Happy Fella.*

Words by Mack Gordon; Music by Edmund Goulding

A small ca-fé, Mam'-selle, Our ren-dez-vous, Mam'-selle, The vi-o-lins were warm and sweet and so were you, Mam'-selle. And as the night danced by, A kiss be-came a sigh. Your love-ly eyes seemed to spar-kle just like

BALLERINA

This song of unrequited love was such a smash that it had two hit recordings to its credit, one by the great Nat Cole — after his days of singing and playing piano with his King Cole Trio — and the other by Vaughn Monroe. Monroe, who started out to be an opera singer, possessed a big, booming baritone voice. Some harsh critics likened it to that of a deep-throated moose. But if the critics

didn't care for him, audiences certainly did all during the 1940s, giving Vaughn tremendous record successes like "My Devotion" and "There, I've Said It Again." His salad days as a record-seller ended just after the decade did, and Vaughn became the commercial spokesman for RCA, the company that owned the label for which he had been such a standout.

Words by Bob Russell; Music by Carl Sigman

Moderate Latin feel

mp

Dance, bal-le-ri — na,
Whirl, bal-le-ri — na,

dance,
whirl,

And do your pir-ou — ette In rhy-thm with your
And just ig-nore the chair That's emp-ty in the

ach-ing heart.
sec-ond row.

Dance, bal-le-ri — na,
This is your mo — ment,

dance;
girl,

You must-n't once for — get A danc-er has to
Al-though he's not out there Ap-plaud-ing as you

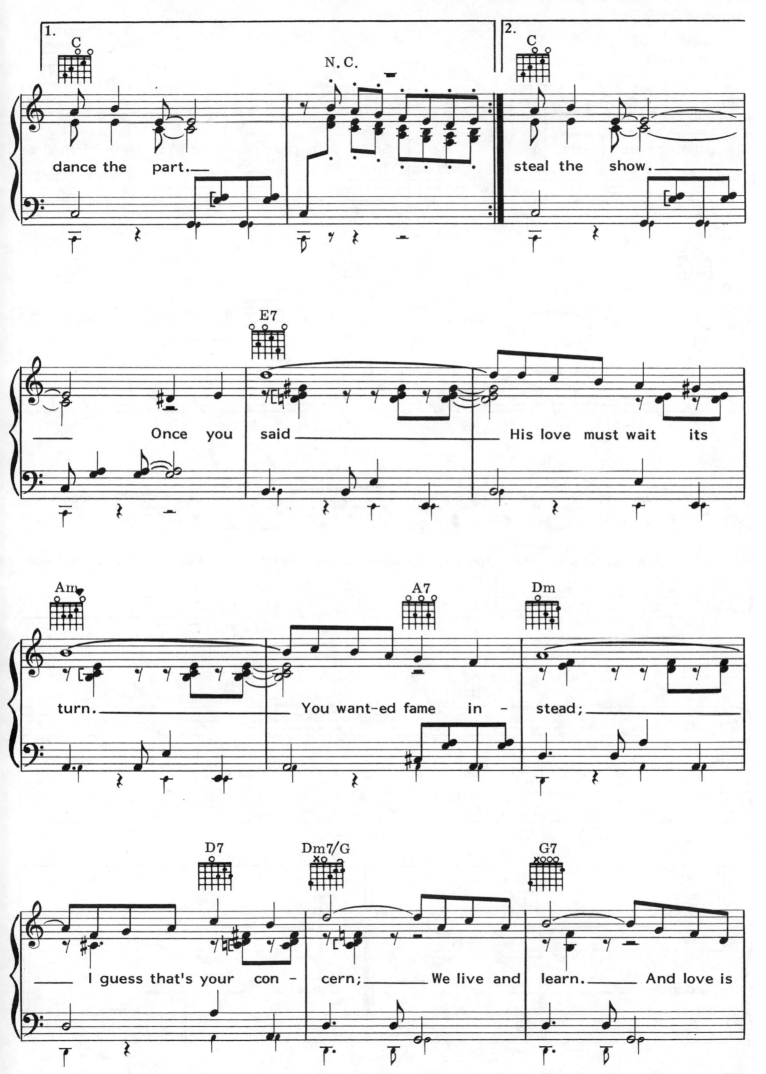

BALLERINA

gone, bal-le-ri – na, gone, So on with your ca – reer; You can't af-ford a

back-ward glance. Dance on and on and on;

A thou-sand peo-ple here Have come to see the show As round and round you

go, So bal-le-ri – na dance, dance,

1. dance. (D.C.) 2. dance.

138

SATURDAY NIGHT

During World War II, many songs aimed themselves directly at the loneliness of soldiers, sailors and marines abroad and their wives and sweethearts back home. This is one of those songs. No doubt, former GIs, now graying at the temples and spreading out somewhat in the middle, still recall listening to "Saturday Night (Is the Loneliest Night in the Week)" on the post exchange jukebox, or a jukebox in a bar or Elks Club in the town next to their camp, and fighting to hold back the tears. The tune

was one of the early successes of the songwriting team of Sammy Cahn and Jule Styne, who had many hits together. Going their separate ways, Styne had a tremendous career on Broadway (including *Gypsy*), and Cahn was equally successful in Hollywood, where he teamed up with Jimmy Van Heusen for many Frank Sinatra hits. Both men had a most productive relationship with Sinatra, who recorded "Saturday Night" in New York in November 1944 and saw (and heard) it become a winner.

(IS THE LONELIEST NIGHT IN THE WEEK)

Words by Sammy Cahn; Music by Jule Styne

SATURDAY NIGHT (IS THE LONELIEST NIGHT IN THE WEEK)

140

BECAUSE OF YOU

Here's a tune that came out in 1941, scored a mild success and then pulled a Judge Crater — it disappeared from the scene. But unlike the judge, "Because of You" reappeared in 1951 and became a tremendous success, largely because of a recording by Tony Bennett, the first of his many great hits. How great a hit was the song? During the late summer and fall of 1951, it was No. 1 on *Your Hit Parade* 11 times in a row. As a matter of fact, it was also No. 2 on six occasions and among the Top 10 from July 21 until December 27, 1951 — continuously. "Because of You" bobbed up in a couple of nonmusical films in 1951. It was interpolated in *I Was an American Spy* and served as background music for *Let's Make It Legal*.

Words and Music by Arthur Hammerstein and Dudley Wilkinson

BECAUSE OF YOU

The conventional wisdom is that the great songs were written in the 1930s and 1940s, and, in terms of volume, this is true. However, there were some lovelies in the 1950s, too. "Ruby" is certainly one of them. It was used as background music for the movie *Ruby Gentry,* which starred Jennifer Jones and Charlton Heston. The melody, written by Heinz Roemheld, a veteran of Hollywood scores, proved so haunting that Mitchell Parish added words to it, and "Ruby" became one of the biggest hit songs of 1953, finally topping at No. 2 on *Your Hit Parade* in the summer of that year. Les Baxter recorded it in his usual lush instrumental style. Like many songs that big, "Ruby" had a second life as a hit when Ray Charles recorded it in 1960.

Words by Mitchell Parish; Music by Heinz Roemheld

MY ONE AND ONLY LOVE

This exquisite song was written by two longtime denizens of Tin Pan Alley: Robert Mellin, who wrote the words, and Guy Wood, who composed the music. When this writer first came to New York in 1954, I met Mr. Wood in the Brill Building. He had arrived in the United States some years earlier from his native England. We wrote a song together called "One Day in Marseilles," and, although it was never recorded, I can still hear his lovely melody to it. Guy Wood is one of those songwriters whose output is small in quantity but high in quality. In addition to "My One and Only Love," he wrote one of the most haunting songs of World War II — "Till Then," one of those tunes that addressed itself directly both to the soldiers overseas and to their friends and loved ones back home.

Words by Robert Mellin; Music by Guy Wood

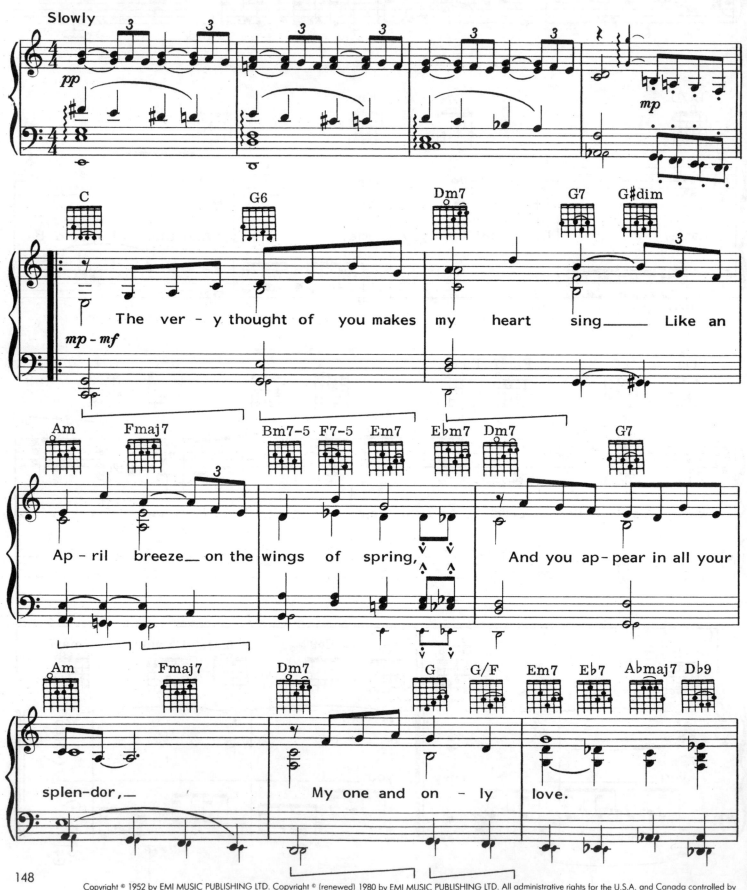

148

The shad-ows fall and spread their mys-tic charms__ In the hush of night__ while you're

in my arms; I feel your lips so warm and ten-der,__

My one and on - ly love. The touch__ of your hand__ is like

heav-en,__ A heav - en that I've__ nev-er known. The

EBB TIDE

If you think you hear harps when you listen to "Ebb Tide," you're absolutely right. Robert Maxwell, its composer, was a harpist par excellence, and he himself once recorded the tune. The lyrics, which seem to fit the melody perfectly, were written by Tin Pan Alley veteran Carl Sigman. "Ebb Tide" was one of the big hits of 1953, with three hit recordings — an instrumental by Frank Chacksfield and vocal versions by Roy Hamilton and Vic Damone. The song was revived in 1966 by The Righteous Brothers, and Frank Sinatra had an excellent outing with it in his album *Only the Lonely*.

Words by Carl Sigman; Music by Robert Maxwell

EBB TIDE

(PUT ANOTHER NICKEL IN)
MUSIC! MUSIC! MUSIC!

Teresa Brewer came singing out of Toledo, Ohio, in time to have a big hit record on the charts for her 19th birthday, May 7, 1950. The song was "Music! Music! Music!," and it immediately established Teresa as a recording star. The record splashed out of jukeboxes and radio sets all during the spring and into the summer of that year. Hits, and the way we remember them, are curious things. Teresa went on to have several huge successes, including "Till I Waltz Again with You" and "Ricochet," and under the aegis of her record executive husband, Bob Thiele, she blossomed into a nifty jazz-oriented vocalist in the 1980s. But, in the way that things happen in the wonderful, crazy world of music, music, music, she will always be best remembered for the hit she had when she turned 19.

Words and Music by Stephan Weiss and Bernie Baum

Little Things Mean a Lot

Pretty Kitty Kallen flirted with fame for a decade before really crashing through in the 1950s. After a stint with Jack Teagarden's band, she sang at radio station WSM in Nashville. Although WSM is justly famous for being the home of *The Grand Ole Opry*, in the 1940s it was also a hotbed of mainline popular music. Kitty later served a tour of duty with Harry James and shared the hit recording of "I'm Beginning to See the Light" with the maestro. It is for her own hit records of the 1950s, however, that she is best remembered. "Little Things Mean a Lot," in 1954, was her biggest success. The song holds a special *Hit Parade* record: Three times it fell out of the top spot and three times it regained it.

Words and Music by Edith Lindeman and Carl Stutz

156 ❋ *sing an 8va lower till* ❋

BE MY LOVE

Mario Lanza burst upon the music scene like a rocket — a giant rocket, to be sure. Born in 1921, he died in 1959 at the age of 38, a victim of his own flamboyance. Into those too-brief years he packed a lot of living and a lot of singing, some of it very good. Perhaps his high-water mark was the 1950 film *The Toast of New Orleans,* in which he costarred with Kathryn Grayson in the role of a fisherman who becomes an opera star. One of the songs in the film was the soaringly beautiful "Be My Love." Lanza's recording sold 2 million copies and is said to be the only RCA Victor Red Seal release (Red Seal is the company's serious music label) to achieve the status of hit song.

Words by Sammy Cahn; Music by Nicholas Brodszky

Freely and rhapsodically

Be my love   For no one else can

end   this yearn - ing,   This need that you and you a-

lone   cre - ate.   Just fill my arms   The way you've

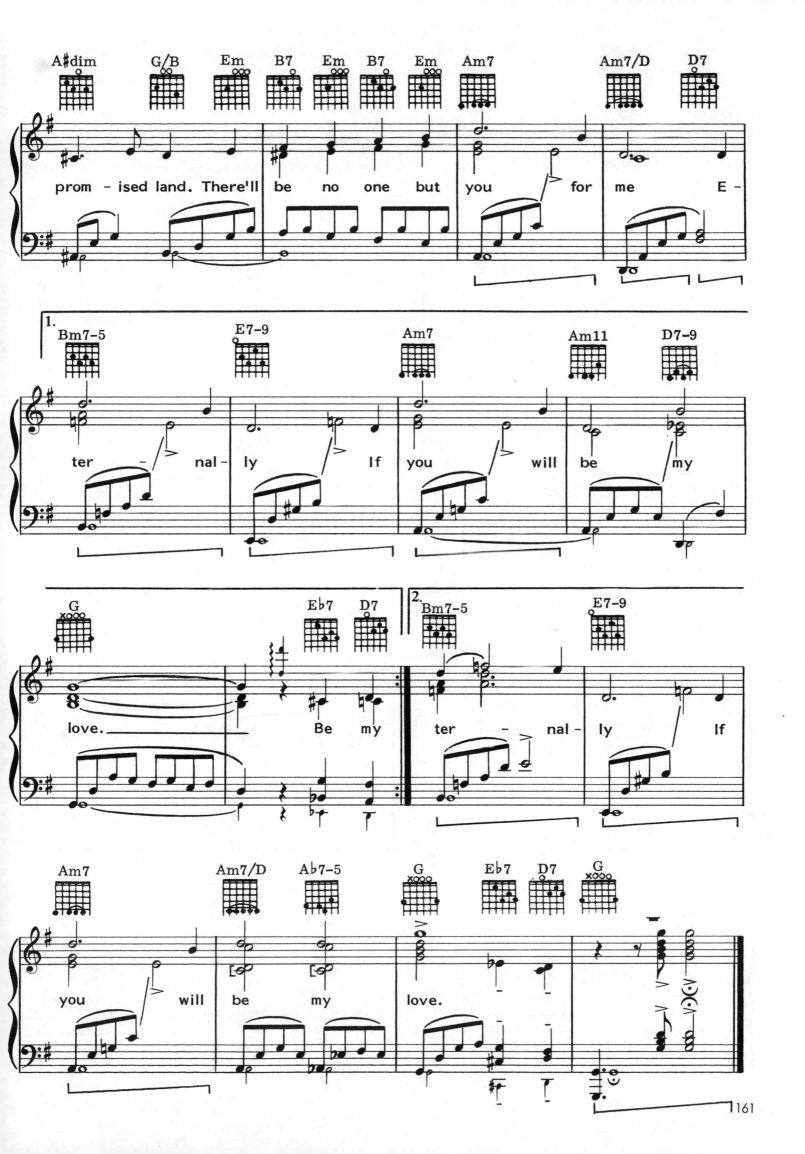

All My Love

This song was born in France, the offspring of Maurice Ravel's "Boléro." An adaptation — also called "Boléro" and having to do with the dance of that name — was made in England; its success, however, was short-lived. But then Mitchell Parish added an entirely new set of lyrics and came up with "All My Love." Patti Page's recording was a smash, reaching No. 1 in October 1950. If additional evidence were needed, this song — along with the many others for which Mitchell provided lyrics — is certainly proof that words are just as important as music.

English words by Mitchell Parish; French words by Henri Contet; Music by Paul Durand

Moderate bolero tempo

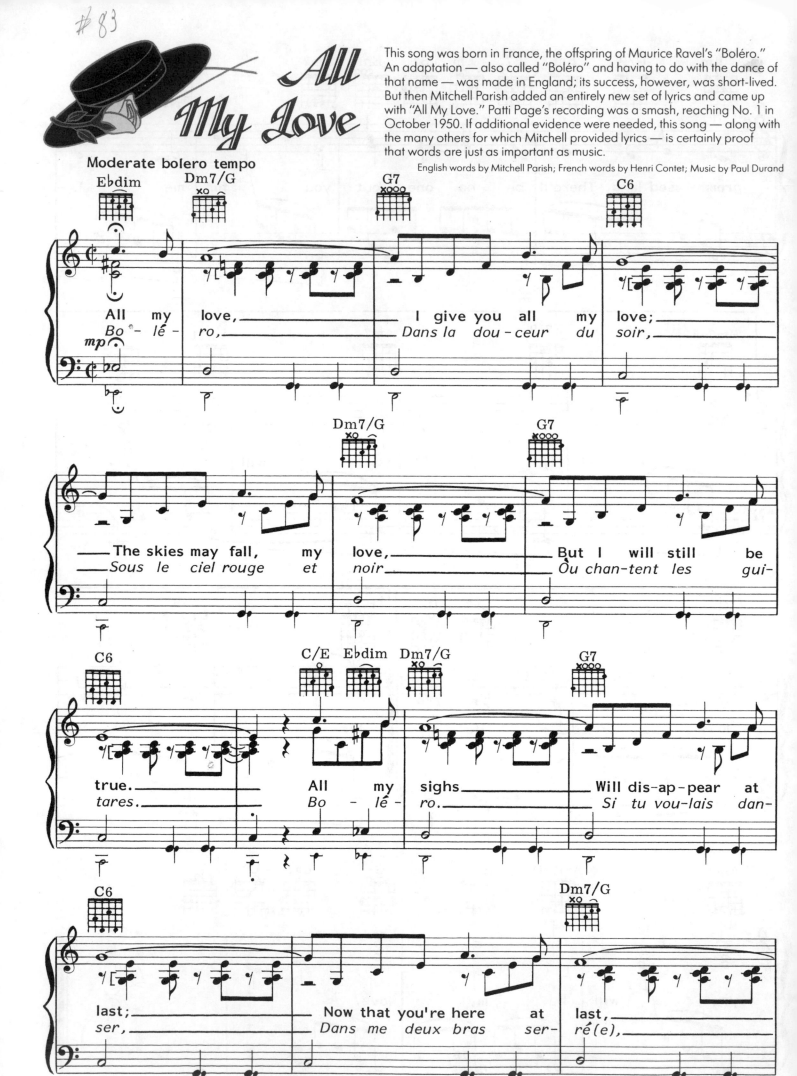

All my love, I give you all my love;
Bo - lé - ro, *Dans la dou-ceur du soir,*

The skies may fall, my love, But I will still be
Sous le ciel rouge et noir *Où chan-tent les gui-*

true. All my sighs Will dis-ap-pear at
tares. *Bo - lé - ro.* *Si tu vou-lais dan-*

last; Now that you're here at last,
ser, *Dans me deux bras ser-ré(e),*

ALL MY LOVE

life____ to give you all my love. Ay, ay,
jour____ Ou j'ai dan-sé L'a-mour. Aïe, aïe,

ay, Ay, ay, ay, Ay, ay, ay. Ay, ay, ay. *very steady*
aïe, Aïe, aïe, aïe, Aïe, aïe, aïe. Aïe, aïe, aïe.

to Verse

1.

2.

ay, Ay, ay, ay._____
aïe, Aïe, aïe, aïe._____

Fine

Brisk tango tempo

Verse

Bow, ca-bal-ler-o, and tip your som-bre-ro To your se-no-ri - ta, the
Comme en un rê-ve la nuit qui se lè-ve Al-lume u-ne flam - me au
p gradually getting louder (mp) (mf)

A GUY IS A GUY

A New York music publisher once asked Oscar Brand whether any of the folk songs he knew might have popular appeal. "Well, just maybe," said the Canadian-born folksinger-songwriter, and he proceeded to rewrite a few of them. One result was "A Guy Is a Guy," based on a folk song that has been around for a long, long time — always with the same theme, but usually with a bawdier treatment. One version appeared in 1719 as "A Knave Is a Knave" in a collection of songs by the English dramatist and songsmith Thomas d'Urfey. And during World War II, soldiers sang "A gob [sailor] is a slob in every degree." And then came Brand's version. It was a smash hit for Doris Day in 1952.

Words and Music by Oscar Brand

I walked down the street like a good girl should. He
(1) stepped to my door like a good girl should. He

fol - lowed me down the street like I knew he would. Be-cause a
stopped____ at my door like I knew he would. Be-cause a

IF I GIVE MY HEART TO YOU

In the 1930s and early 1940s, a song could, and frequently did, make *Your Hit Parade* without benefit of a hit recording. Movie musicals and network radio exposure often were enough. But by September of 1954, when "If I Give My Heart to You" made its first appearance on the show, five of the seven songs featured were strictly "record hits." (Besides "If I Give My Heart to You," these were "Sh-Boom," "The Little Shoe-maker," "Skokiaan" and "They Were Doin' the Mambo"). And the other two songs — "The High and the Mighty" and "Hey, There" — although from Hollywood and Broadway respectively, depended on recordings for their popularity. "If I Give My Heart to You" gained its hit status thanks to a best-selling recording by Doris Day.

Words and Music by Jimmie Crane, Al Jacobs and Jimmy Brewster

#92   102   29

During the golden age of Hollywood films, there were three songs in particular that Metro-Goldwyn-Mayer got a lot of mileage out of. One was the title song of *The Broadway Melody*, and another was "You Were Meant for Me," also from the 1929 movie; the third was "Singin' in the Rain." In addition to appearing in several more musicals, the tunes were used frequently in trailers and puff pieces for the studio. All three songs were written by the vastly underrated team of Nacio Herb Brown and Arthur Freed, who also gave us "Temptation," "All I Do Is Dream of You" and "You Are My Lucky Star." Freed became head of the musical wing of MGM and turned out some excellent films, including *Singin' in the Rain,* in which many of the Brown-Freed songs appeared.

YOU WERE MEANT FOR ME

From *The Broadway Melody*

Words by Arthur Freed;
Music by Nacio Herb Brown

Nice and easy

You were meant for me,

I was meant for you.

175

MORE Than You Know

New York-born Vincent Youmans lived only 47 years, and, though he continued to write, published nothing after his excellent score for Hollywood's *Flying Down to Rio* in 1933, when he was only in his mid-30s. Plagued by illness for years, he died in Denver, Colorado, in 1946. According to associates, he was not a self-promoter in any sense of the word. (A recent biography recounts that he talked Louis B. Mayer out of filming his life story.) At times a heavy drinker — and tubercular to boot — he is said to have frequently neglected his health. But just take a look at a few of the lovelies he created during his short career: Besides "More Than You Know," they include "Tea for Two," "I Want to Be Happy," "Sometimes I'm Happy," "Without a Song" and "Time on My Hands." "More Than You Know" is one of Youmans' prettiest songs. And what a fine verse!

From *Great Day*   Words by Billy Rose and Edward Eliscu; Music by Vincent Youmans

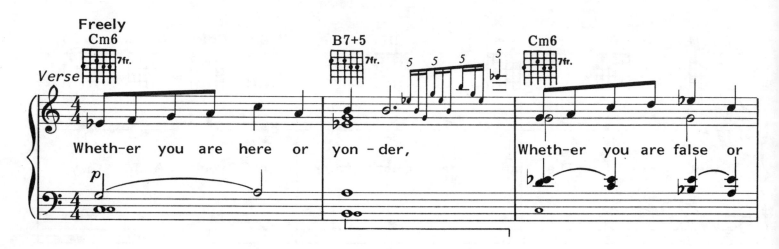

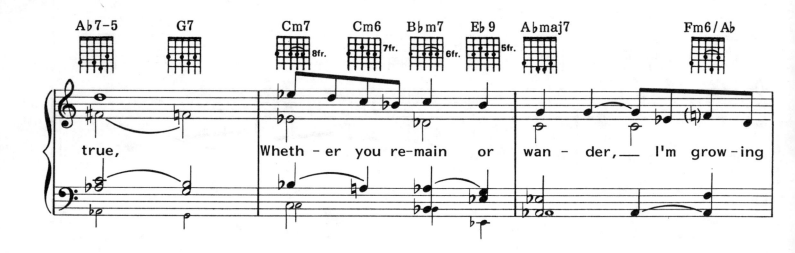

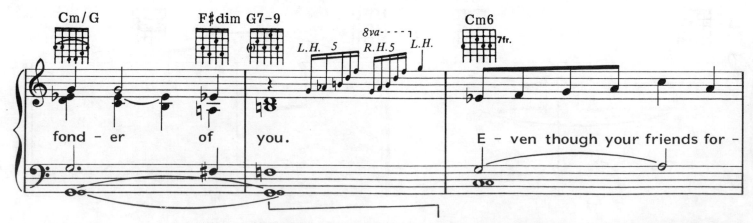

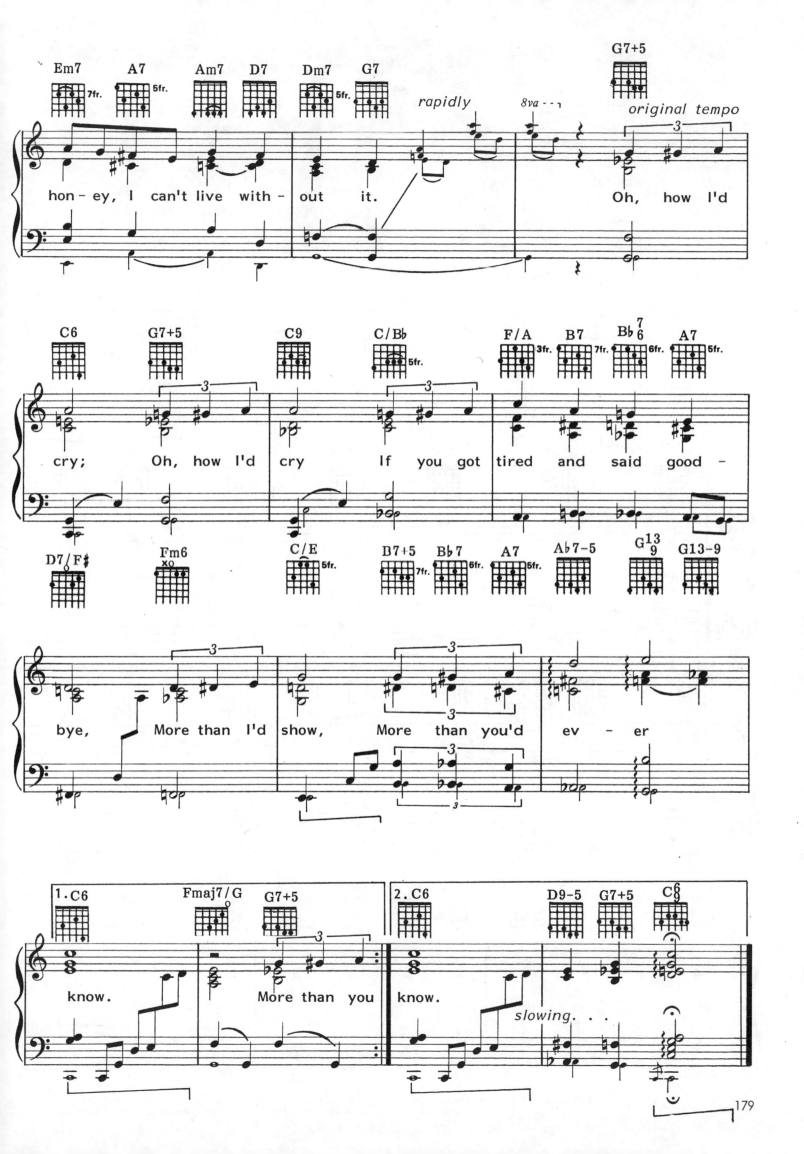

I MARRIED AN ANGEL

Between the years 1937 and 1942, Richard Rodgers and Lorenz Hart turned out a dazzling array of hit Broadway shows — *I'd Rather Be Right, Babes in Arms, The Boys from Syracuse, Pal Joey, By Jupiter* and, one of 1938's brightest moments, *I Married an Angel*. The last play became a screen vehicle for Jeanette MacDonald and Nelson Eddy, but somewhere between coasts it got mangled, and it turned out to be a heavy-footed swan song for the two as a team. The musical's title song is a lovely, bright and breezy Rodgers and Hart effort, with the typical AABA formula, in which the theme appears and is repeated once; then a "bridge," or middle part, appears; and then the theme returns — with perhaps a slightly altered ending.

From *I Married an Angel*

Words by Lorenz Hart;
Music by Richard Rodgers

Slowly and rather freely

A FINE ROMANCE

Fred and Ginger. Ginger and Fred. Only Amos 'n' Andy and Franklin and Eleanor rival them when it comes to summing up in two names the United States of the 1930s. Strangely enough, RKO's original teaming of the pair in 1933 in *Flying Down to Rio* (they had second billing to Gene Raymond and Dolores Del Rio) was more or less accidental. But by the time they filmed *Swing Time* three years later, Fred and Ginger were Hollywood's No. 1 duo and a staggering success. *Swing Time,* with a hit-laden score by the great Jerome Kern and Dorothy Fields, is in many people's opinion the best of the nine films that the twosome made together. One of the highlights was the etched-in-irony song "A Fine Romance."

From *Swing Time*　　Words by Dorothy Fields; Music by Jerome Kern

Bright and bouncy

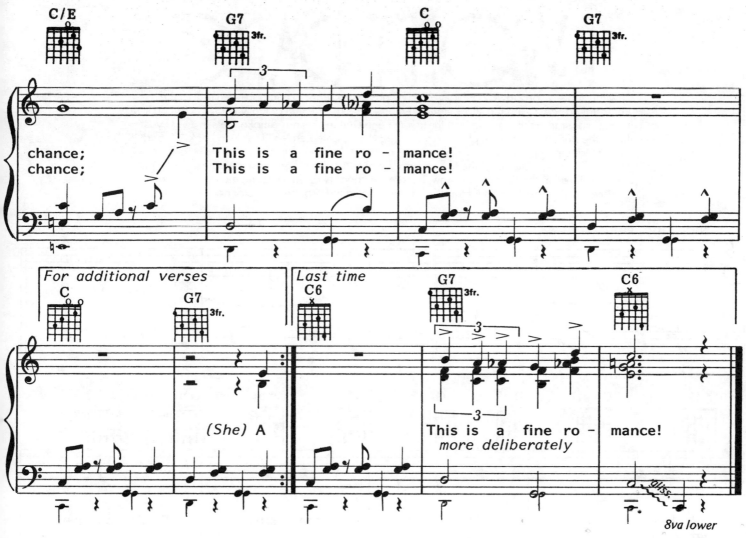

For additional verses

Last time

(She) A

This is a fine ro - mance!
more deliberately

8va lower

Fred's Lyrics

A fine romance
With no kisses!
A fine romance,
My friend, this is!
We two should be like clams in a dish of chowder,
But we just fizz like parts of a Seidlitz powder.
A fine romance
With no clinches,
A fine romance
With no pinches.
You're just as hard to land as the *Ile de France*!
I haven't got a chance;
This is a fine romance!

A fine romance,
My dear Duchess!
Two old fogies
Who need crutches!
True love should have the thrills that a healthy crime has.
We don't have half the thrills that *The March of Time* has!
A fine romance,
My good woman,
My strong
Aged-in-the-wood woman!
You never give the orchids I send a glance;
No, you like cactus plants.
This is a fine romance!

I WON'T DANCE

Few musicals — Broadway *or* Hollywood — possess a score to compare with that of the immortal *Roberta*. And the show stands almost alone as one that actually *improved* when it was filmed. For starters, the movie had the lovely Irene Dunne singing "Smoke Gets In Your Eyes" (from the Broadway score), plus two new songs by Jerome Kern — "Lovely to Look At" and "I Won't Dance." And it boasted Hollywood's greatest dancing team, Fred Astaire and Ginger Rogers. The only criticism of the film version is that two of Kern's greatest melodies, songs that were featured in the Broadway show, became secondary or background music. They are the lovely "The Touch of Your Hand" and the devastating "You're Devastating."

From *Roberta*

Words by Dorothy Fields and Jimmy McHugh; Music by Jerome Kern

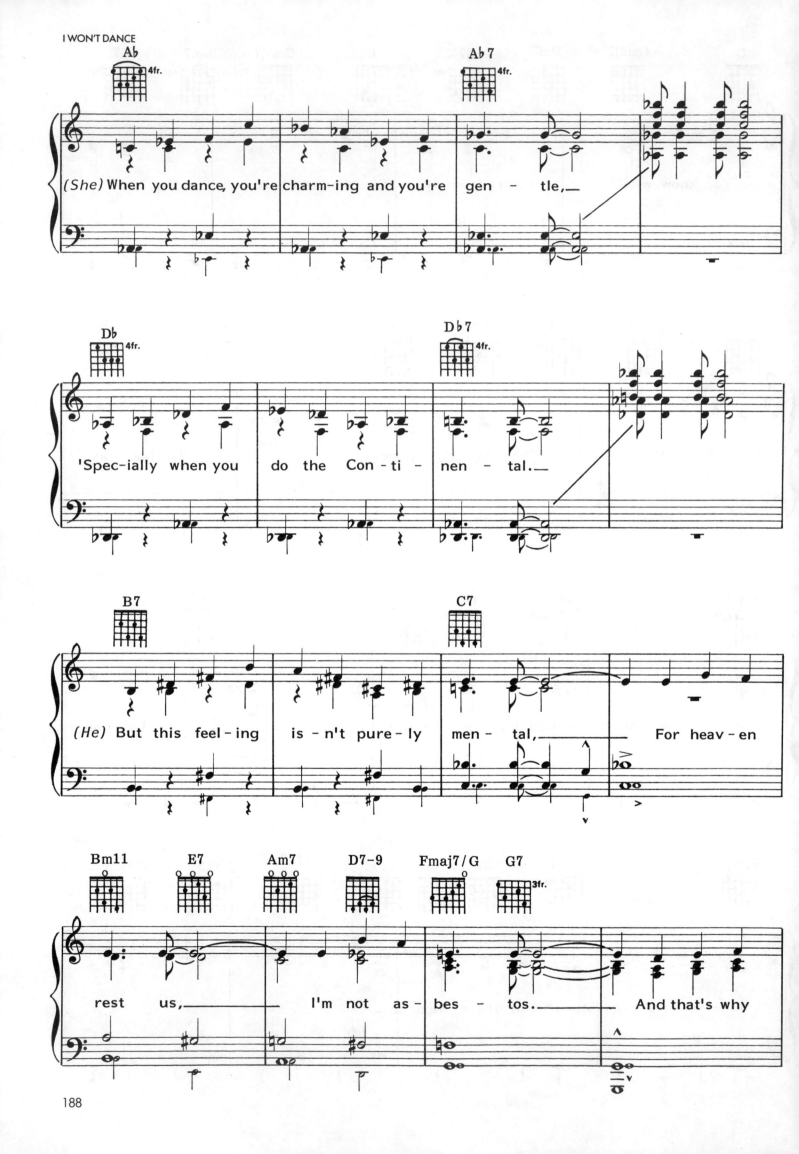

WHEN I'M WITH YOU

In 1936, Shirley Temple was in trouble everywhere except at the box office. That year she was a "stowaway" in the movie of that name and a runaway in *Poor Little Rich Girl*. Coincidentally, the wonderful Alice Faye appeared in both films. In *Poor Little Rich Girl*, Alice is the distaff side of a vaudeville team — Jack Haley is her partner — and it is with them that Shirley runs away. The other team represented here, that of songwriters Mack Gordon and Harry Revel, turned out hit after hit in just a half-dozen years together, most of them songs of the highest quality. Just look at a few: "Did You Ever See a Dream Walking?," "May I?," "Stay As Sweet As You Are," "Good Night, My Love" (see page 193), "The Loveliness of You" and this pretty tune from *Poor Little Rich Girl*.

From *Poor Little Rich Girl*   Words and Music by Mack Gordon and Harry Revel

With a lilt

Ev-'ry street I walk on be-comes a lov-ers' lane When I'm with you...

I can see the sun though we're out in the rain

When I'm with you.

To lose you would be trag-ic;

GOOD NIGHT, MY LOVE

By the time Twentieth Century-Fox cast Shirley Temple in *Stowaway*, the eight-year-old was, despite her age — or maybe because of it — queen of the silver screen. "Good Night, My Love," from *Stowaway*, is a lovely song by Mack Gordon and Harry Revel, who wrote a lot of good tunes at Fox for Shirley, Alice Faye, Tony Martin, Sonja Henie and others. Gordon went on to an even bigger second career at the same studio, collaborating with Harry Warren. This writer used Shirley Temple's recording of "Good Night, My Love" as his signature theme for many years on radio. The song was also recorded on the Victor label — in the same year as the movie, 1936 — by a very young Ella Fitzgerald with Benny Goodman.

Slowly and somewhat freely

From *Stowaway*   Words and Music by Mack Gordon and Harry Revel

TWO SLEEPY PEOPLE

After appearing on Broadway in *Roberta* and *The Ziegfeld Follies of 1936*, Bob Hope proceeded to Hollywood, where he launched his film career with *The Big Broadcast of 1938*. He scored so heavily with the film's Academy Award-winning song "Thanks for the Memory" that Paramount cast him in a movie called *Thanks for the Memory*, with the same co-star, Shirley Ross. This time Bob and Shirley were tossed an excellent tune by Hoagy Carmichael and Frank Loesser: "Two Sleepy People." In addition to being a comedic superstar, Hope introduced — or co-introduced — an amazing array of songs. Besides the above, they include "Personality," "Silver Bells," "Buttons and Bows" and "Road to Morocco." And here's a shocker. Although "I Can't Get Started" was made famous by bandleader Bunny Berigan, do you know who introduced it? That's right. Our boy Bob, in the aforementioned *Ziegfeld Follies of 1936*. And try this on for trivia size. He sang it with Eve Arden.

From *Thanks for the Memory*   Words by Frank Loesser; Music by Hoagy Carmichael

THAT OLD BLACK MAGIC

During World War II, the major Hollywood studios, in a fit of patriotism, outdid each other in making all-out-for-the-war-effort movies that were loaded with stars doing specialty numbers. Such films, in fact, usually contained practically all of the contract players on the lot. There was, for instance, *Stage Door Canteen*, with fabled names dancing or pouring coffee and serving donuts. Warner Brothers really got carried away and gave us two: *Thank Your Lucky Stars* and *Hollywood Canteen*. To his everlasting credit, although he appeared in *Thank Your Lucky Stars*, Humphrey Bogart refused to sing. Paramount, not to be outdone, gave us a 1942 extravaganza called *Star Spangled Rhythm*, with everybody from Bing Crosby to Vera Zorina putting in an appearance. It was Zorina who danced to this great song, while Johnny Johnston sang it. Through the years, "That Old Black Magic" became a staple in Billy Daniels' act, and it even survived an onslaught by Louis Prima and Keely Smith, in 1958.

From *Star Spangled Rhythm*   Words by Johnny Mercer; Music by Harold Arlen

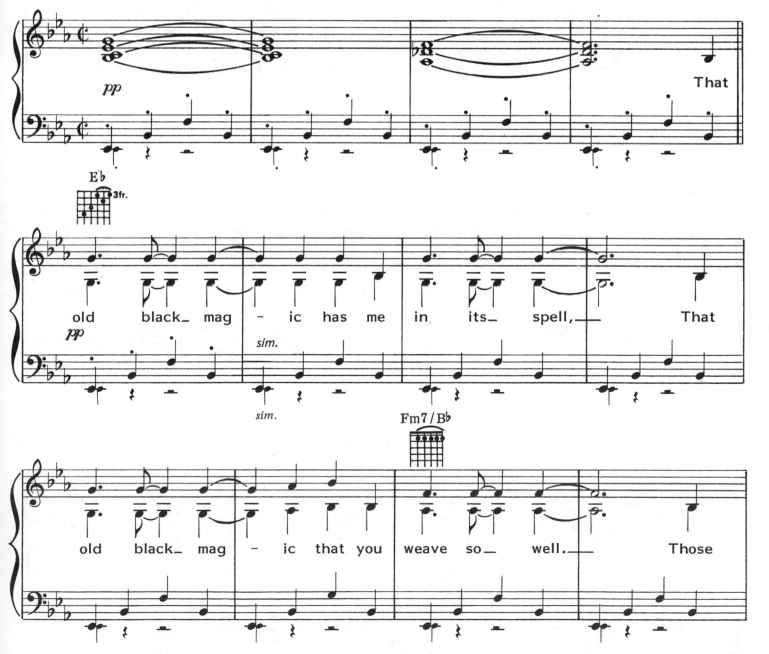

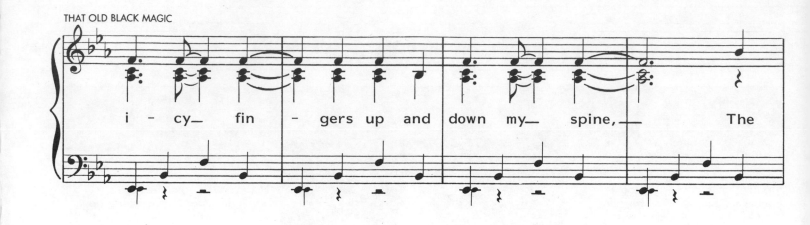

i - cy_ fin - gers up and down my_ spine,_ The

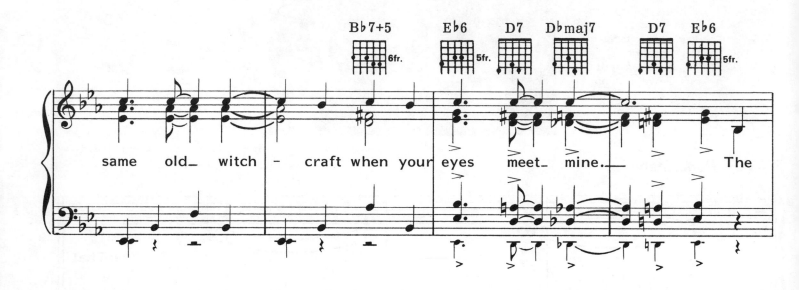

same old_ witch - craft when your eyes meet_ mine._ The

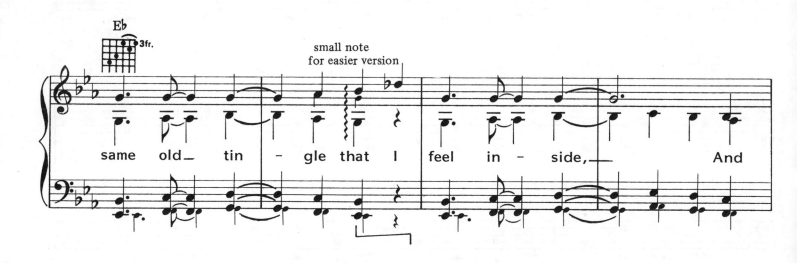

same old_ tin - gle that I feel in - side,_ And

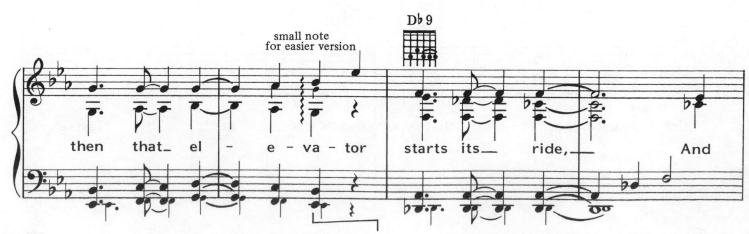

then that_ el - e - va - tor starts its_ ride,_ And

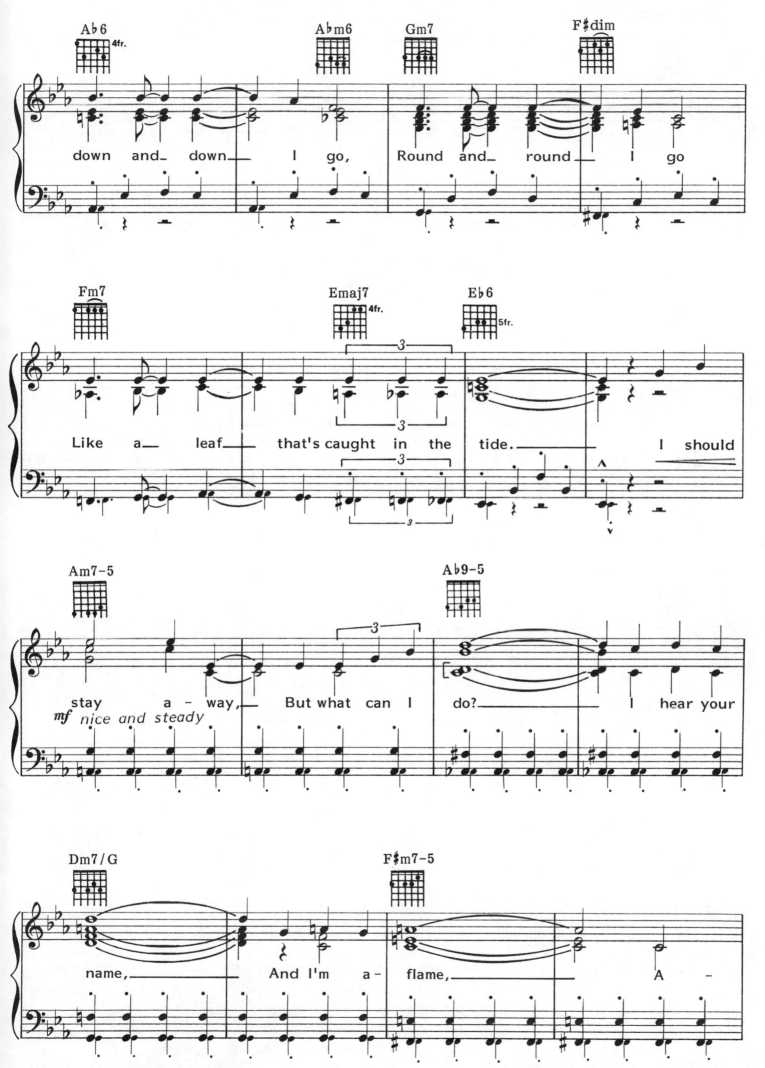

This strong song appeared in a 1948 film called *Road House,* a nasty piece of business involving a sadistic club owner played by Richard Widmark. (The movie also starred Ida Lupino, Cornel Wilde and Celeste Holm.) It doesn't seem to be by accident that "Again" is from the movie, because it has a definitely torch-songy, long-about-midnight sound to it, dark without being somber, sophisticated without being arch. As a Top 10 tune, the song threatened never to die, appearing in the select circle in all or part of five straight months. Such was its staying power that it hit the No. 1 spot twice, three weeks apart.

From *Road House*   Words by Dorcas Cochran; Music by Lionel Newman

TAKING A CHANCE ON LOVE

Of all the major American popular-song composers, perhaps Vernon Duke is the least known. Born Vladimir Dukelsky in Russia, he arrived in the United States after a spell in Paris. Although not as prolific as, say, Cole Porter or Jerome Kern, he gave us some exquisite songs, including "I Can't Get Started," "April in Paris," "Autumn in New York," "What Is There to Say" and the delightful score for *Cabin in the Sky,* which hit Broadway in 1940 and left behind the lovely title tune and this evergreen. One of the show's stars was Dooley Wilson, who scored a couple of years later as Sam, the pianist in *Casablanca.* Speaking of films, *Cabin in the Sky* was made into one in 1943. And a very good one, too. Along with the celebrated Ethel Waters, Eddie Anderson — who gained immortality as Jack Benny's "Rochester" — turned in an excellent performance. Curiously, a good song was added to the film, but Vernon Duke didn't write it. It was Harold Arlen and E. Y. Harburg who contributed "Happiness Is a Thing Called Joe."

From *Cabin in the Sky*   Words by John Latouche and Ted Fetter; Music by Vernon Duke

MY DARLING, MY DARLING

After a most fruitful decade and a half in Hollywood, Frank Loesser arrived on Broadway in 1948 — and he arrived triumphantly. *Where's Charley?*, for which he wrote both the words and music, was a musical adaptation of Brandon Thomas's *Charley's Aunt,* a turn-of-the-century comedy. The show starred Ray Bolger, one of the most famous dancers of the time, and was a personal success for him as well as for Loesser. *Where's Charley?*, whose score also included "Once in Love with Amy" (see page 212), paved the way for such later Loesser shows as *Guys and Dolls, The Most Happy Fella* and *How to Succeed in Business Without Really Trying.*

From *Where's Charley?*   Words and Music by Frank Loesser

ONCE IN LOVE WITH AMY

If ever there was a showstopper, folks, this was it. "Once in Love with Amy" stopped the 1948 Broadway musical *Where's Charley?* dead in its tracks nightly. Not only that, the audience sang along. Ray Bolger didn't complain. The producers didn't complain. *Nobody* complained. Why should they? The show became famous because of the song. Unlike many Broadway musicals, the stage show transferred beautifully to the screen, in 1952, with its star intact. As we've noted earlier, *Where's Charley?* was based on the comedy *Charley's Aunt,* which was originally made into a film — starring Jack Benny posing as the old aunt — in 1941. Bolger, through the years, appeared in several movies (including, of course, his role as the Scarecrow in *The Wizard of Oz,* in 1939) but was never as successful or as good as he was on Broadway in such shows as *Where's Charley?, On Your Toes* and *By Jupiter.* His soft-shoe style did not move as gracefully to the screen as that of Fred Astaire or Gene Kelly, and, unfortunately, he was not the leading-man type. But for all of that, he certainly gave fans their money's worth, on Broadway and in Hollywood.

From *Where's Charley?*   Words and Music by Frank Loesser

"Buttons and Bows" is from a Paramount film called *The Paleface* and won the Oscar for Best Song of 1948. *The Paleface,* sort of a friendly send-up of Westerns, co-starred the voluptuous Jane Russell as Calamity Jane, doing the shooting for Bob Hope, who played a dentist named (jokingly, after a Los Angeles disc jockey) Painless Peter Potter. Dinah Shore made the big hit record of "Buttons and Bows."

From *The Paleface*   Words and Music by Jay Livingston and Ray Evans

Medium bounce

East is east   and
bur - y me   in

west is west, And the wrong one I have chose;
this prai-rie; Take me where the ce-ment grows;

Let's go where you'll (I'll)
Let's move down to

keep   on   wear-in' Those frills and   flow-ers and but-tons and bows,
some   big   town Where they   love   a   gal by the   cut o' her clothes, And

Rings   and things and but-tons and   bows.
you'll (I'll) stand out in   but-tons and   bows.

Don't

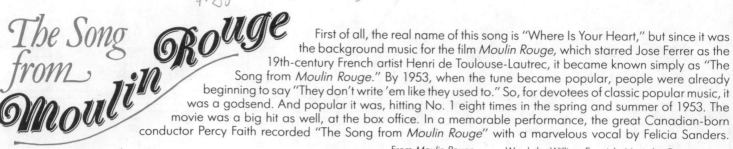

The Song from Moulin Rouge

First of all, the real name of this song is "Where Is Your Heart," but since it was the background music for the film *Moulin Rouge,* which starred Jose Ferrer as the 19th-century French artist Henri de Toulouse-Lautrec, it became known simply as "The Song from *Moulin Rouge.*" By 1953, when the tune became popular, people were already beginning to say "They don't write 'em like they used to." So, for devotees of classic popular music, it was a godsend. And popular it was, hitting No. 1 eight times in the spring and summer of 1953. The movie was a big hit as well, at the box office. In a memorable performance, the great Canadian-born conductor Percy Faith recorded "The Song from *Moulin Rouge*" with a marvelous vocal by Felicia Sanders.

(Where Is Your Heart)

From *Moulin Rouge*   Words by William Engvick; Music by Georges Auric

LET'S GET LOST

After a fabulously successful career at Warner Brothers, from about 1933 to 1939, Dick Powell found himself floundering. Tenors, seemingly, were somewhat out of favor. In 1940, Preston Sturges cast him in a hilarious film called *Christmas in July*, but there didn't seem to be any follow-up. In 1944, Dick found his way to a new non-singing career when he played the tough Los Angeles detective Philip Marlowe in *Murder My Sweet*. In between was a film at Paramount called *Happy Go Lucky*, in which he co-starred with Mary Martin and Betty Hutton. *Happy Go Lucky* is seldom seen these days, but it did give us one lasting memory, this very sophisticated and pretty tune, written by two of Hollywood's greatest and most prolific songwriters, Frank Loesser and Jimmy McHugh.

From *Happy Go Lucky*   Words by Frank Loesser; Music by Jimmy McHugh

Moderate and smooth

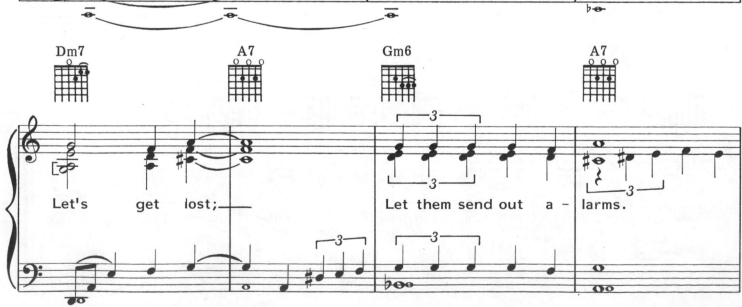

LET'S GET LOST

This is the title song from a 1957 movie that starred Shirley Jones and a young man named Charles Eugene "Pat" Boone, a direct descendant of Daniel. Pat Boone was one of the major recording stars of the 1950s, starting with his first record, "Two Hearts," in 1955. A sort of squeaky-clean alternative to Elvis Presley, Pat in short order became a semi-regular on television and radio with Arthur Godfrey, and also in the movies. The year 1957 was probably his biggest. He starred in two movies, *April Love* and *Bernadine,* and was all over the record charts with the title songs from the two films and two other recordings that went to Nos. 1 and 2, respectively — "Love Letters in the Sand" and "Don't Forbid Me." Amazingly for that era, none of the songs was really rock and roll, and "Love Letters in the Sand" was over 25 years old. Naturally, nobody told Pat's teenage fans. Two decades later, his daughter Debby had a No. 1 hit with "You Light Up My Life."

APRIL LOVE

From *April Love*   Words by Paul Francis Webster; Music by Sammy Fain

Slowly and rhapsodically

April love Is for the very young;—

Ev - 'ry star's a wish-ing star that shines for you.

APRIL LOVE

first bou - quet. But A - pril

love Can slip right through your fin - gers, So if

she's the one, Don't let her run a - way.

1.

2.

way.

Something's Gotta Give

Fred Astaire made nine movies with Ginger Rogers. But he also appeared in a number of films with many other dancing ladies, some much better than others. Among his partners were Joan Crawford, Joan Fontaine, Eleanor Powell, Judy Garland, Cyd Charisse, Joan Caulfield and Leslie Caron — the last in *Daddy Long Legs,* which gave us "Something's Gotta Give," written by Johnny Mercer. *Daddy Long Legs* has to do with a French orphan who is provided for by a rich single man, whose identity is unknown to her. The picture was not well received, but it did give Fred a chance to go into his dance, and with a very talented co-star at that.

From *Daddy Long Legs*   Words and Music by Johnny Mercer

Medium swing

pp cresc.

ff gliss on white keys

Dm7 **G7+5** **Cmaj7**

When an ir - re - sist - i - ble force such as you___
When an ir - re - press - i - ble smile such as yours___

Dm7 **G9** **Fm/C** **Cmaj7**

Meets an old___ im - mov - a - ble ob - ject like me,___
Warms an old___ im - pla - ca - ble heart such as mine,___

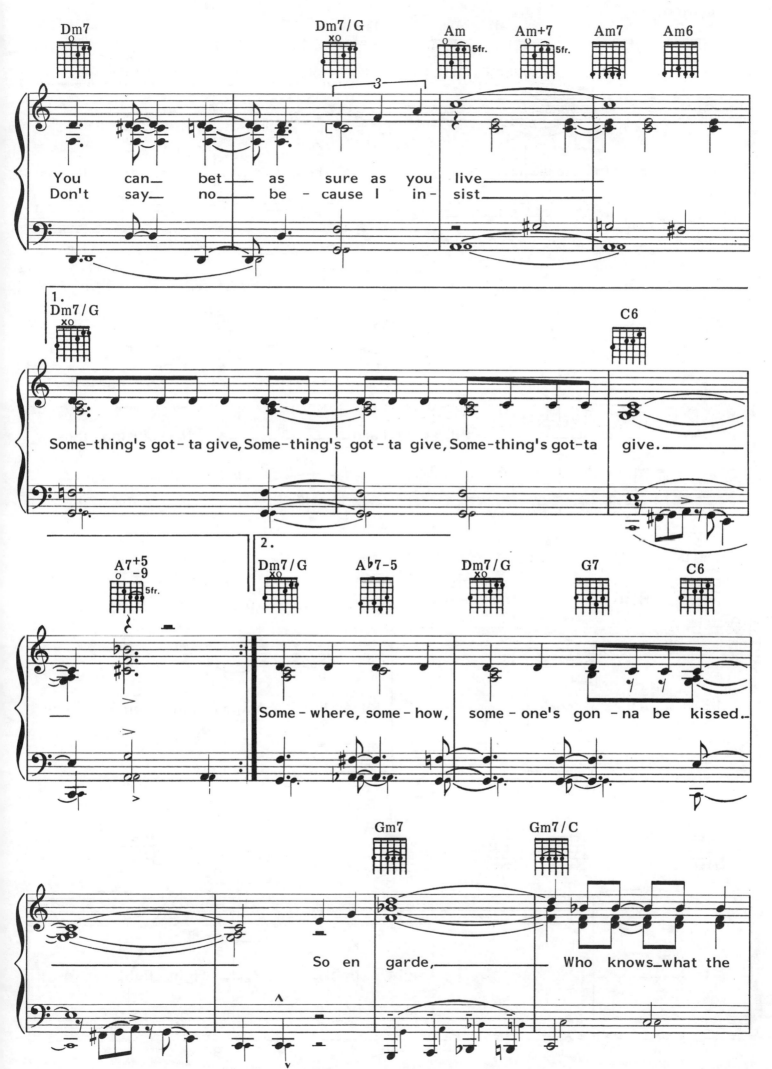

8va lower

229

THE ABA DABA HONEYMOON

"The Aba Daba Honeymoon," which has been around since 1914, is a carryover from the great days of vaudeville. It was introduced at the mecca of vaudeville in the United States, the Palace in New York City, by a star of the medium named Ruth Roye. Through the years, kids have sung the song around campfires, and it has had almost as many revivals as Billy Graham. Paul Whiteman, known as The King of Jazz, pumped it back up in 1930 in a movie called, of all things, *The King of Jazz*. MGM revived it in the film *Two Weeks with Love*, released in 1950 and set in the Catskills. But the biggest impetus — probably the reason why most of us remember the tune today — was the hit record by Debbie Reynolds and Carleton Carpenter, who were featured in *Two Weeks with Love*.

Words and Music by Arthur Fields and Walter Donovan

Brightly, with manic humor

see note below

"Ab-a, dab-a, dab-a, Dab-a, dab-a, dab-a, dab," Said the chimp-ie to the *sim.* monk. "Bab-a, dab-a, dab-a, Dab-a, dab-a, dab-a, dab," Said the

Note: For easier performance, keyboard players may play this and analogous passages as

230

I Wanna Be LOVED

"I Wanna Be Loved" was written by three men — Edward Heyman, Billy Rose and Johnny Green — who are responsible for a slew of major standards. Heyman, a lyricist, wrote the words for such evergreens as "Love Letters," "When I Fall in Love" and "Boo-Hoo!" Among the credits of legendary producer-entrepreneur-writer Billy Rose are the words to "I Found a Million Dollar Baby," "Me and My Shadow" and "It's Only a Paper Moon." Johnny Green, musical arranger and composer, in collaboration with Heyman, wrote some of the greatest songs of all time, including "Body and Soul," "I Cover the Waterfront" and "Out of Nowhere." The Andrews Sisters rescued "I Wanna Be Loved" from near obscurity and gave it new life in 1950, two decades after it was introduced at Billy Rose's nightclub, Casino de Paree, in New York City.

Words by Billy Rose and Edward Heyman; Music by Johnny Green

THINKING OF YOU

This "Thinking of You" (another song of that name was Kay Kyser's theme) was written by Bert Kalmar and Harry Ruby, who also gave us such standards as "Who's Sorry Now?," "Nevertheless" and "Three Little Words." It was introduced in *The 5 O'Clock Girl*, a 1927 musical, and was prominently featured in *Three Little Words*, the 1950 film biography of Kalmar and Ruby that starred Fred Astaire and Red Skelton. A hit recording of the song by Eddie Fisher followed in short order that same year.

Words by Bert Kalmar; Music by Harry Ruby

Why____ is it I spend the day,
Why____ does it do this to me;
____ Wake up and end the day____ Think-ing of you?____
____ Is it such bliss to be____ Think-ing of you? And when I fall a-

I'm Confessin'
(That I Love You)

Words by Al. J. Neiburg; Music by Doc Dougherty and Ellis Reynolds

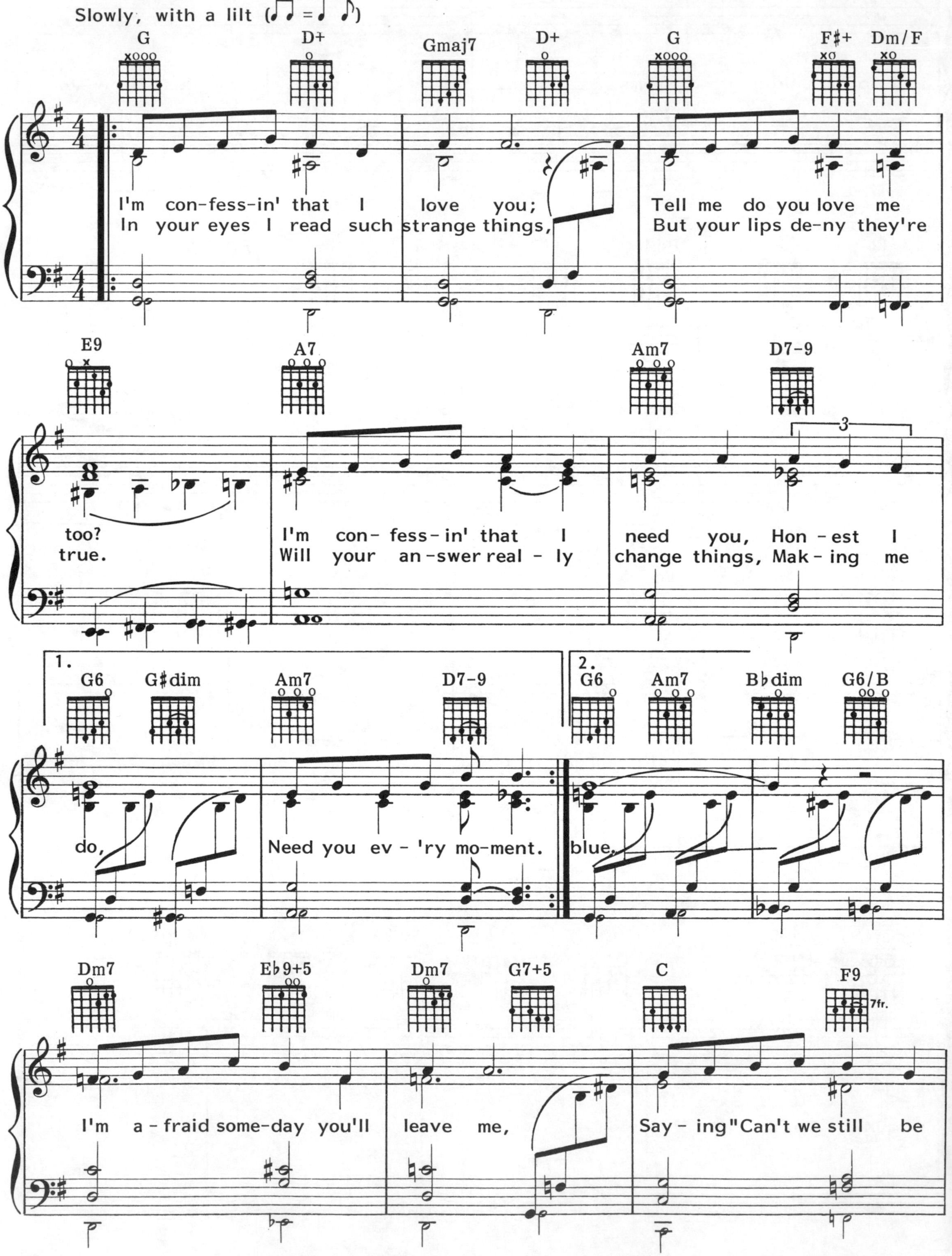

Slowly, with a lilt
G D+ Gmaj7 D+ G F♯+ Dm/F
I'm con-fess-in' that I love you; Tell me do you love me
In your eyes I read such strange things, But your lips de-ny they're
E9 A7 Am7 D7-9
too? I'm con-fess-in' that I need you, Hon-est I
true. Will your an-swer real-ly change things, Mak-ing me
1. G6 G♯dim Am7 D7-9
do, Need you ev-'ry mo-ment.
2. G6 Am7 B♭dim G6/B
blue.
Dm7 E♭9+5 Dm7 G7+5 C F9
7fr.
I'm a-fraid some-day you'll leave me, Say-ing "Can't we still be

This song has a history as slippery as an eel. In its original form it was called "Lookin' for Another Sweetie" and was recorded by the legendary Thomas "Fats" Waller in 1929. Then, as "Confessin'," it was recorded by Louis Armstrong in 1930, and the fact that the song has always been considered a jazz classic probably has its roots in Louie's rendition. (Joe Williams later made an excellent recording of the tune with the Count Basie band.) It has been a major standard since the 1930s, and through the years it came to be called "I'm Confessin' (That I Love You)." In that incarnation, the song enjoyed a renaissance when Perry Como recorded it in the fall of 1944. It was one of Perry's first hits, preceding even his gigantic smash, "Till the End of Time."

I'll Never Say "Never Again" Again

This song is one of the few to contain a quote within its title. "I'll Never Say 'Never Again' Again" first saw the light of day in 1935, and it was a big light, too. The song reached the hit parade in the summer of that year and made a great impression. It was written by a man named Harry Woods, who wrote several of the most successful tunes of the 1930s, including "We Just Couldn't Say Good-bye," "Try a Little Tenderness" and "A Little Street Where Old Friends Meet" — not to mention Kate Smith's theme,

"When the Moon Comes Over the Mountain." Woods is but little remembered today, probably because he had no Broadway or Hollywood connection. Dinah Shore had a hit with "I'll Never Say 'Never Again' Again" in 1957. Benny Goodman has always been associated with the song, although he did not record it until 1953, when, at a recording session that reunited some of the original members of the Goodman band, he cut an excellent disc of it with Helen Ward, his first girl vocalist.

I Wonder Who's KISSING Her Now

"I Wonder Who's Kissing Her Now" has an interesting background. Four men are listed as its composers: Will Hough, Frank R. Adams, Joseph E. Howard and Harold Orlob. Lyricists Hough and Adams aren't the interesting part of the story. The song was introduced in 1909 by Joseph Howard, a songwriter and vaudevillian, and over time became Howard's most durable piece. In 1947, "I Wonder Who's Kissing Her Now" gave its name to a fictionalized account of the songwriter's life. Harold Orlob, whose name did not appear on the song originally, had been saying for years that he was the real writer. When the movie was released, Orlob had had all he could take. He filed suit in court against Howard, not for money but simply to receive credit for the work. He won. Justice triumphed.

Words by Will Hough and Frank R. Adams;
Music by Joseph E. Howard and Harold Orlob

won-der who's kiss-ing her now._____ I won-der who's teach-ing her how._____ I won-der who's look-ing in-to her eyes, breath-ing sighs, tell-ing

I'm Nobody's Baby

Words and Music by Benny Davis, Milton Ager and Lester Santly

When movie musicals became big, some of the major studios went into the music-publishing business. Paramount had its own firm, the company called Famous Music. Warner Brothers purchased three of the largest in Witmark, Harms and Remick. MGM did the same thing, buying up Robbins, Feist and Miller. So, in addition to their own staffs of songwriters, Warners and MGM had access to music catalogues that dated back to the time of World War I. Quite often, they would delve into their vast holdings to find a good song for a particular movie sequence or star, and frequently they would come up with just the ticket. This was certainly the case with "I'm Nobody's Baby," which MGM chose for Judy Garland to sing in the 1940 film *Andy Hardy Meets a Debutante*. The song, from the catalogue of Leo Feist, had been written in 1921 by Benny Davis, Milton Ager and Lester Santly. As teenage Hardy fans returned to high school in the fall of 1940, the 19-year-old song was young all over again.

MAYBE

"The second time around" may be stretching it just a bit for "Maybe," because the song hardly had a first time around when it debuted in 1935. But "Maybe," written by Allan Flynn and Frank Madden, certainly made the grade the second time around, no maybes about it. It shot all the way to No. 1 on *Your Hit Parade* and stayed there for several weeks in the fall of 1940. As was the case with so many other songs of the 1940s and '50s, the success of "Maybe" was due to a recording

Words and Music by Allan Flynn and Frank Madden

by The Ink Spots. Bill Kenny's name might not have been well known by itself, but everybody knew the sound of that falsetto tenor voice in the group. His sound was a familiar one indeed, for two decades. "Maybe" was a hit the third time around, too — thanks to a 1952 recording by Perry Como and Eddie Fisher. For the record, this "Maybe" is one of five ASCAP songs with that title. One of them was composed by the great George Gershwin.

MY IDEAL

Words by Leo Robin; Music by Richard A. Whiting and Newell Chase

There's a touching story behind this song. It was written in 1930 for Maurice Chevalier by Leo Robin and Richard Whiting. Shortly before his death in 1937, at the all-too-early age of 46, Whiting teamed up with Johnny Mercer. In the last year of Whiting's life, the pair wrote "Hooray for Hollywood" and "Too Marvelous for Words," among other fine songs. Mercer later became a founder of Capitol Records, and one of the first artists he signed was the 17-year-old daughter of the late Richard Whiting. For her first record he chose her father's "My Ideal." With it, in 1943, Margaret Whiting gave Johnny the first of many hits she would make for him and Capitol.

Slowly, with a lilt

Will I ev-er find The {girl / boy} in my mind,— The one who is my_ i-deal? May-be {she's / he's} a dream And yet {she / he} might be_ Just a-round the cor-ner wait-ing for me.—

Twilight Time

Back in the early 1940s, the instrumental-vocal combo The Three Suns shone brightly from a bistro in New York's theater district, the reason being that the NBC radio network used to pick them up for 15 minutes nationwide nearly every afternoon. Two of The Three Suns (brothers Al and Morty Nevins) wrote their theme, "Twilight Time," along with Buck Ram, the trio's arranger. ("I'll Be Home for Christmas" is among his other compositions.) Well, some years later Buck was managing and conducting for The Platters. After The Platters' big success with "My Prayer," they were looking for material, and Buck just happened to remember "Twilight Time." And a good thing too, because, in 1958, "Twilight Time" became a big hit all over again.

Words by Buck Ram; Music by Morty Nevins and Al Nevins

Heav – en – ly shades of night are fall – ing, It's twi – light time.
Deep – en – ing shad – ows gath – er splen – dor As day is done.

Out of the mist your voice is call – ing, It's twi – light time.
Fin – gers of night will soon sur – ren – der The set – ting sun.